A

ARTHUR HUGH CLOUGH

ARTHUR HUGH CLOUGH

A MONOGRAPH

BY

SAMUEL WADDINGTON

LONDON: GEORGE BELL AND SONS
YORK STREET, COVENT GARDEN
1883

CHISWICK PRESS :—C. WHITTINGHAM AND CO., TOOKS COURT,
CHANCERY LANE.

εἰσέτι γὰρ πνείει τὰ σὰ χείλεα
        καὶ τὸ σὸν ἄσθμα,
ἀχὼ δ᾽ ἐν δονάκεσσι τεὰς
        επιβοσκετ᾽ ἀοιδάς.

MOSCHUS.

PREFACE.

IN preparing the following study of Clough's life and poems I have more especially availed myself of the information contained in the notices, reviews, and other fugitive papers respecting him, which have been published during the last quarter of a century ;—and, with a view of preserving all that might prove of interest, numerous extracts have been included from the writings of various authors, who were, for the most part, personally acquainted with the poet. Among such writers may be mentioned the late Dean of Westminster, Mr. R. H. Hutton, Mr. Matthew Arnold, the late Mr. Walter Bagehot, the Dean of St. Paul's, Mr. F. T. Palgrave, Mr. Thomas Hughes, Q.C., Professor Masson, Mr. William Allingham, Professor Sellar, Mr. J. A. Symonds, Mr. C. E. Norton, Mr. T. Arnold, Professor Shairp, the late Charles Kingsley, and others.

The present would appear to be a period unusually productive as regards the publication of monographs and biographies, and in the case of one poet—Shelley—there have been, if I remember rightly, nearly a dozen critical and biographical works published in rapid succession within a very few years. This is, however, the first volume that has been devoted to the criticism and study of Clough, although nearly a quarter of a century has now elapsed since he was laid in the 'little cypress-crowded cemetery beyond the walls of the Fair City (Florence), on the side towards Fiesole.'—The 'sincerity and sense,' which, with a rare Homeric simplicity of genius, are the characteristic features of Clough's poetry, will, I trust, impart an interest and value to the present volume which it might not, perhaps, otherwise have possessed.

I would take this opportunity of thanking Mrs. Clough, and also Messrs. Macmillan and Co., for their kindness in granting me permission to print extracts from the poet's works.

47, Connaught Street,
    Hyde Park, W.
        October, 1882.

CONTENTS.

INTRODUCTION.

IT has been said that 'poets are all who love, who feel great truths and tell them,'—and we know that of old ' they were ranked in the class of philosophers, and that the ancients made use of them as preceptors in music and morality.' But now, in these latter days, *nous avons changè tout cela*, and we look to the ministers of religion, to our pastors and masters, to preach and teach us morality; while we expect our bards, or singers (as some of them now prefer to be called), to teach us something quite different,—or rather we expect them not to teach at all. And yet, as a matter of fact, all classes are being taught, and cannot fail to be taught, by those verses which, when once read, remain stamped on the tablets of memory for life : and it was not unwisely written by Andrew Fletcher, of Saltoun, in a letter to the Marquis of Montrose, that 'if a man were permitted to make all the ballads, he need not care who should make the laws of a nation.' The influence of the poetry of Robert Burns in forming and colouring the opinions and characters of his countrymen is said to have been greater than that of any other Scotchman of his century ;—and the influence of Keats, a poet of a very different order, is plainly perceptible at the present time in England, and is affecting many sections of society, and more especially the art and literary circles of the metropolis. A few years ago the same might have been observed, with equal truth, respecting Wordsworth ; but it is to the author of *Endymion* and *The Eve of St. Agnes* that reference is usually made by those modern critics who extol what they themselves call 'mere poetry,' although it was Keats that complained of those who forget

'the great end
Of Poesy, that it should be a friend
To soothe the cares, and lift the thoughts of man.'

And yet if this is what is meant by 'mere poetry,' if it means verse that 'lifts the thoughts of man,' and makes us feel

'that we are greater than we know,'

then it becomes clear that the contention respecting it is only a dispute about words, and arises from the fact that our two schools of criticism do not quite understand each other's meaning. The poetry of Burns and of Wordsworth, or even that of Shakspeare and of Milton, can hardly be said to do more than 'soothe the cares, and lift the thoughts of man;' and we are not prepared to say that the poetry of Keats at all fails to accomplish the like end. The lines

> 'Beauty is truth, truth beauty,—that is all
> Ye know on earth, and all ye need to know,'

contain the one 'great truth' which Keats loved, and felt, and taught; and which coloured, and in a measure consecrated, all his compositions. Never was there a philosopher who was more firmly attached to his own particular views respecting the world in which he moved, nor ever a preceptor whose example was more in accordance with his teaching.

Still, all this notwithstanding, it seems probable, seeing that the minds of men are differently constituted, and variously influenced by imagination and reason, by thought and emotion, that there will

ever be found in our midst these two schools holding opposite views respecting the province and
proper sphere of poetry. The one delights, and
will always continue to delight, in the form, the
manner, the music, the metaphor, the graceful
phrase, the uncommon, the well-chosen or, perhaps,
archaic term, and all the thousand-and-one adjuncts
that go to form the dress in which the poet clothes
his thought,—or, alas, in some instances conceals
his want of thought. The other school also delights
in all these things ;—it rejoices in the harmonious
arrangement of words, and in the subtle felicity of
expression ;—it loves

> ' the light that never was on sea or land ; '

but these, these alone, these unaccompanied by any
deep ' under-song of sense,' are not sufficient for
it, and it asks, ' Is not the body more than raiment,
and the soul of more importance than the body ? '

> ' Why dost thou pine within and suffer dearth,
> Painting thy outer walls so costly gay ? '

Or, in the words of Isaac Barrow, it exclaims : ' If it
is true that nothing has for you any relish except
painted comfits and unmeaning trifles, that not even
wisdom will please you, unless without its peculiar

flavour, nor truth, unless seasoned with a jest, then in an unlucky hour have I been assigned as your purveyor, neither born nor bred in such a frivolous confectionery.'

Such, roughly and briefly stated, are the two opposite views that are held by the respective partisans and upholders of the especial value in poetry of form and manner, on the one hand, and of thought and subject-matter, on the other:—but it is in the latter rather than the former of these schools that the poet who is the subject of these pages has for the most part found his disciples and admirers. Those who cherish, and find pleasure in studying the writings of Clough—and we believe that their number, both in this country and in America, is much larger than is usually supposed—admire him, not for the smoothness of his numbers, or the melody of his verse, but for the nobility of character, the subtlety of thought, and the sincere earnestness and zeal in the pursuit of both truth and truthfulness, that are marked in no uncertain letters upon all his compositions, whether in prose or verse. As regards the question, however, respecting the province of poetry, to which reference has already been made, it will be well before proceeding to the study of the poet's own writings that some insight should, if possible, be obtained into what were the opinions which he himself held on this subject. With this view the following interesting extract is quoted from a paper published by him in the *North American Review* for July, 1853, in which he reviewed and compared the respective poems of the late Alexander Smith and Mr. Matthew Arnold. He writes :—

'We have before us, we may say, the latest disciple of the school of Keats, who was indeed no well of English undefiled, though doubtless the fountain-head of a true poetic stream. Alexander Smith is young enough to free himself from his present manner, which does not seem his simple and natural own. He has given us, so to say, his *Endymion ;* it is certainly as imperfect, and as mere a promise of something wholly different, as was that of the master he has followed. We are not sorry, in the meantime, that this *Endymion* is not upon Mount Latmos. The natural man does pant within us after *flumina silvasque ;* yet really, and truth to tell, is it not, upon the whole, an easy matter to sit under a green tree by a purling brook, and indite pleasing stanzas on the beauties of nature and fresh air? Or is it, we incline to ask, so very great an exploit to wander out into the pleasant field of Greek or Latin mythology, and reproduce, with more or less of modern adaptation,

> 'the shadows
> Faded and pale, yet immortal, of Faunus, the Nymphs, and the Graces?'

Studies of the literature of any distant age or country; all the imitations and *quasi*-translations which help to bring together into a single focus the scattered rays of human intelligence; poems after classical models, poems from Oriental sources, and the like, have undoubtedly a great literary value. Yet there is no question, it is plain and patent enough, that people much prefer *Vanity Fair* and *Bleak House.* Why so? Is it simply because we have grown prudent and prosaic, and should not welcome, as our fathers did, the Marmions and the Rokebys, the Childe Harolds and the Corsairs? Or is it, that to be widely popular, to gain the ear of multitudes, to shake the hearts of men, poetry should deal, more than at present it usually does, with general wants, ordinary feelings, the obvious rather than the rare facts of human nature ? Could it not attempt to convert into beauty and thankfulness, or at least into some form and shape, some feeling, at any rate, of content—the actual, palpable things with which our every-day life is concerned ; introduce into business and weary task-work a character and a soul of purpose and reality ; intimate to us relations which, in our unchosen, peremptorily-appointed posts, in our grievously narrow and limited spheres of action, we still, in and through all, retain to some central, celestial fact ? Could it not console us with a sense of significance, if not of dignity, in that often dirty, or at least dingy, work which it is the lot of so many of us to have to do, and which some one or other, after all, must do ? Might it not divinely condescend to all infirmities ; be in all points tempted as we are ; exclude nothing, least of all guilt and distress, from its wide fraternization ; not content itself merely with talking of what may be better elsewhere, but seek also to deal with what *is* here ? We could each one of us, alas ! be so much that somehow we find we are not ; we have all of us fallen away from so much that we still long to call ours. Cannot the Divine Song in some way indicate to us our unity, though from a great way off, with those happier things; inform us, and prove to us, that though we are what we are, we may yet, in some way, even in our abasement, even by and through our daily work, be related to the purer existence.'

Thus writes, and very wisely, the poet himself,— and it is both surprising and instructive to note, as the eye passes along the eloquent and impassioned sentences, how closely the sense, the gist of the whole passage, approximates to those words of Keats, to which reference has been made, that the great end and aim of poetry should be 'to soothe the cares and lift the thoughts of man.' The very fact that two poets, such as were Keats and Clough, whose compositions are in many respects so very dissimilar,—who in seeking a field in which the poetic genius might work and develop its powers to advantage, turned their backs upon each other, and parted at the very threshold,—who travelled, or seemed to travel, on their respective paths in quest of apparently very different objects of desire,—that these two poets should nevertheless agree on this important subject, and should hold like views respecting the fundamental principle of what should be the great end of poetry, is, to say the very least of it, instructive, and a matter which should not be overlooked by our youthful bards and modern reviewers.

There have recently been various theories propounded respecting what may best serve as a true definition of 'poetry;'—and while Mr. Matthew Arnold tells us that it is the *criticism* of life, Mr. Alfred Austin intimates that it is nothing of the kind, but that it is the transfiguration or imaginative *representation* of life. Possibly there is much truth in both of these theories, and yet, after all, may we not say in the words of Wordsworth,—

> ' Dear child of Nature, let them rail !
> —There is a nest in a green dale,
> A harbour and a hold,
> Where thou * * * shalt see
> Thy own delightful days, and be
> A light to young and old.'

And may not these lines, also, serve in a measure to indicate one phase at least of what poetry either is, or ought to be ? But so long as the term is widely and variously employed, as it is at present, it is manifestly a waste of time to try and include under one definition its manifold and various meanings. Originally it would appear to have meant rhythmical compositions, or creations, of any kind or character; and a century ago it would have been considered applicable to what we should now only deem to be correctly described as ' verse : '—while it would not have been held to be an appropriate term for any composition in prose, even if written by such imaginative or emotional writers as Thomas Carlyle and Mr. Ruskin.

The ' poetry of life ' is plainly far removed from the poetry (if there be any) in Pope's *Essay on Man*, or Samuel Butler's *Hudibras :*—while the poetry that Wordsworth could find in ' a primrose by a river's brim,' or in his favourite, ' the lesser celandine,' is an entirely different thing from that which inspires some of Mr. Matthew Arnold's philosophic, didactic, and yet very beautiful ser-mons-in-sonnets, such as are his *East London*, *The Better Part*, and *Worldly Place*. But let us once more refer on this subject to the paper by Clough in the *North American Review* where he writes :—'You have been reading Burns, and you take up Cowper. You feel at home, how strangely ! in both of them. Can both be the true thing ? and if so, in what new form can we express the relation, the harmony, between them ? Are we to try and reconcile them, or judge between them ? May we escape from all the difficulty by a mere quotation, and pronounce with the shepherd of Virgil,

> 'Non nostrum inter vos tantas componere lites
> Et vitulâ tu dignus, et hic.'

* * * * Will you be content, O reader, to plod in German manner over miles of a straight road that seems to lead somewhere, with the prospect of arriving at last at some point where it will divide at equal angles, and lead equally into two opposite directions, where you may therefore safely pause, and thankfully set up your rest, and adore in sacred doubt the Supreme Bifurcation ?'

But now let us consider a moment what is the conclusion at which we are arriving,—what is the end and aim of these introductory observations. Is it to set up, and adore the poetic Supreme Bifurcation, as the poet himself humorously designates the point where the pathways of two schools of poetry divide ? Is it to show that the wonder-working process of Evolution has in its literary progress created at various points of divergence new and distinct species of poetry ? Is it to indicate that whereas one school, or species, will more especially serve ' to soothe the cares,' another will rather 'lift the thoughts,' of Man ? Is it to urge that both of these schools are good in their way, and to be esteemed for their own particular merits ? Is it to prove that of Clough and Keats, as of Cowper and Burns, it may justly be said,

' Et vitulâ tu dignus, et hic ? '

Or, lastly, is it to point out that it is hardly wise in literature—any more than it is in religion—to confine the growing, the ever-increasing world of thought, and truth, and sympathy, by any narrow exclusive dogma, or definition, that may at the time best fit in with our own opinions and predilections ?

Yes—these, taken together, constitute the goal to which our observations tend, for in writing of a poet, such as Clough, who is far removed from the sphere in which the new poets that have arisen during the last fifteen or twenty years are moving, it would seem necessary to point out *in limine* that it does not follow that one is right, and the other wrong, when two poets choose very different methods, and compose poems on opposite principles. There is, after all, much of fashion in these matters, and in addition there is the influence which the events of the period, the religious and political movements of the times, must always have upon the poet's work. It is to this that Mr. Stopford Brooke refers when he writes :—'Keats marks the exhaustion of the impulse which began with Burns and Cowper. There was now no longer in England any large wave of public thought or feeling such as could awaken poetry. We have then, arising after his death, a number of pretty little poems, having no inward fire, no idea, no marked character. They might be written by any versifier at any time, and express pleasant indifferent thought in pleasant verse. But with the Reform agitation, and the new religious agitation at Oxford which was of the same date, a new excitement or a new form of the old, came on England, and with it a new tribe of poets arose, among whom we live. The elements of their poetry were also new, though their germs were sown in the previous poetry. It took up the theological, sceptical, social, and political questions which disturbed England. It gave itself to meta-physics and to analysis of human character. It carried the love of natural scenery into almost every county in England, and described the whole land.

Some of its best writers are Robert Browning and his wife, Matthew Arnold, and Arthur Hugh Clough.'

Of these four only two, unfortunately, are still left with us to work and use their influence in our midst, at a time when their influence is especially needed, and when the school of purely *Decorative Poetry* (to use the late Mr. Bayard Taylor's phrase) which addresses itself to the eye and ear, rather than to the heart and brain, is beginning to somewhat weary its readers. Of Browning and Clough it is especially true that they are 'thinkers' rather than 'singers,' and the following which has been written respecting the former is also true of the latter: 'He as a singer has been surpassed by many inferior men. We had almost said he seldom sings. But he is a poet for all that, and he can sing, and sing sweetly too, when he pleases. But he is chiefly dear to the age as a feeler and a thinker; he is also dear because knowing all, and having been racked with its doubts, and stretched upon the mental torture-wheels of his time, he does not despair.' It is possible that Mr. M. Arnold when he recently defined poetry as the 'criticism of life,' was thinking more especially of these two poets, Browning and Clough, these spiritual analysts of the social body, that unveil the conventional shams of the world, that show us life as it really is, and do not hesitate to criticize our most cherished dogmas of duty and religion. But there is another, and far wider, definition of poetry, given, we believe, by John Stuart Mill, that it is, 'Thought coloured by emotion, expressed in metre :'—and if we accept this as approximately true, then may we accept, also, Clough's compositions as true poetry, for in them we find the most subtle 'thought' accompanied by the most deep and impressive emotion, which is none the less deep and impressive because it is held under restraint, and bears the calm demeanour of discipline. Those who, on bygone Sabbath afternoons, when the shades of approaching darkness began to deepen the gloom of the grand old Abbey, have listened in past years to the touching eloquence and the calm yet impressive language of Arthur Penrhyn Stanley, will recognize at once the same spiritual fervour,—the same earnest, yet restrained, zeal and emotion—in the poems of Clough and the sermons of the late Dean. And, indeed, are not these in a measure but different pipes of the same organ-stop,—are they not fragrant flowers gathered from the same holy garden,—the work

and wisdom of two scholars that had been nurtured
and trained under the fostering care of one and the
same master, that great and good man the late
Dr. Arnold ? Thought, coloured by emotion, yet
subject to discipline ;—sincere earnestness in the
pursuit of Truth coloured by charity towards the
holders of opposite views and opinions ;—a desire to
impart wider views and a larger sympathy to the
various sects of society with their petty shibboleths
and narrow party-spirit ;—such, truly, were the
feelings and the aims that inspired the spiritual
fervour of both poet and priest; and such is the
didactic purpose which we find to be present,
though not objectionably obtruded, in most of the
poems and prose writings of Clough.

A didactic purpose ? Yes,—for when a great
truth has taken possession of the heart,—when an
eternal verity (as Carlyle would have said) hath
entered into and overpowered the spirit of the man,
—then, and then only, out of the fullness of the
heart the mouth speaketh, and teacheth whether
it will or not. Then, and then only, the poet
uttereth such impassioned poems, as *The world is
too much with us, late and soon*, as Hood's *Bridge
of Sighs*, or Mrs. Browning's *Cry of the Children*.

C

But we have already discussed this subject above, and we will not refer to it further, beyond stating that the effect produced by a man who is in earnest will always be greater than that produced by one who is only playing his part ; and that the character of the worker will, in some way or other, be mirrored in the works that he produces. 'Believe me,' were the words of Sir Frederick Leighton on a recent occasion, 'believe me, whatever of dignity, whatever of strength we have within us, will dignify and will make strong the labours of our hands ; whatever littleness degrades our spirit will lessen them and drag them down. Whatever noble fire is in our hearts will burn also in our work, whatever purity is ours will chasten and exalt it ; for as we are, so our work is, and what we sow in our lives, that, beyond a doubt, we shall reap for good or for ill in the strengthening or defacing of whatever gifts have fallen to our lot.' In the following pages the reader will have before him the history of the life, and description of the character, of one whom we, for our part, believe to have been a very pure, and noble, and good man ; he will also have an account and study of his poems and other writings, and he will thus have an oppor-

tunity of judging for himself how very true in this
instance are the words we have here quoted. It
has been said, and with much truth, that 'Clough
lived his poem ;' and his life and poetry are alike
free from any impurity, from any folly or unfaith-
fulness; in neither will the reader come upon any
'deathless traces of a dreadful history,' and they who
have an appetite for—a hungering after—stories of
crime, of desertion and death ;—of poems composed
in the dreamy interregnum of sober moments in
lives of delirious intemperance, whether produced
by alcohol or opium,—must seek their unwholesome
food elsewhere : they will not even meet with any
epistolary compositions unworthy to have been
written by a man of true nobility of character, by a
man of a sane and thorough manliness. And if
Sir Frederick Leighton be right, as we think
he unquestionably is, that 'as we are, so our
work is ;' and that 'whatever purity is ours will
chasten and exalt it,' then may we look for, and
expect with no fear of disappointment, a loftier
spirituality, a higher tone, and a nobler purpose in
the poetry of Clough than in that of the majority
of our English poets. We say, in his words, 'we
could each one of us be so much that some-

how we find we are not; we have all of us fallen
away from so much that we still long to call ours;
cannot the Divine Song in some way indicate to us
our unity, though from a great way off, with these
happier things?' And we reply that such a song
is in a measure to be found in the poetry of many
bards who have indicated, who have shown to us,
our relationship to a purer existence and a happier
state. In the poems of Goethe and Schiller, and
no less in those of our own Spenser and Wordsworth, is such a Divine Song to be traced, such an
echo, as it were, from a more heavenly shore,—a
musical cadence of angels' voices freed from our
earthly bonds, our weakness, and our worldliness,
and, alas! our human worldly-holiness. And not
only in these, but in many others of our English
poets, is such a strain to be found, and in none is it
more marked than in the poetry of Clough; indeed,
as might be expected, it is the main feature of his
verse; it is the light illuminating, more or less
brightly, nearly the whole of his compositions.

The following elegiac lines, which form part of one
of his earlier poems, illustrate to some extent the
general tone and tenor of his poetry, and with them
we will conclude these introductory observations.

'Go from the east to the west, as the sun and the stars
    direct thee,
  Go with the girdle of man, go and encompass the earth.
Not for the gain of the gold ; for the getting, the hoarding,
    the having,
  But for the joy of the deed ; but for the Duty to do.
Go with the spiritual life, the higher volition and action,
  With the great girdle of God, go and encompass the earth.
    *   *   *   *   *

Go with the sun and the stars, and yet evermore in thy spirit
  Say to thyself : It is good : yet is there better than it.
This that I see is not all, and this that I do is but little ;
  Nevertheless it is good, though there is better than it.'

Chapter I.

EARLY LIFE.

IN the year 1819 were born two writers whose characters were in some respects somewhat similar. Both of them were remarkable for their earnestness and integrity, both of them were poets, and both were destined to become disciples and upholders of the Broad-Church school of liberty and free-thought. The one was Charles Kingsley, and the other Arthur Hugh Clough. To the former we shall have occasion to refer later on; the latter forms the subject of these pages. Clough was by a few months the elder of the two, being born on the first day of the new year; and as Heine, who was born in the year 1801, used to jest about himself as being one of the *first men of his century*, so of Clough it may be said that he was one of the first men of his year. He was, in truth, a 'New Year's gift,' and rarely have parents been honoured with a goodlier one, or with one fated to give them more pleasure in the brief after-years of their lives.

It has long been generally recognized, and is almost a truism, that in the majority of cases the men who have become illustrious in the world's history, and of these more especially the poets, have been the sons, if not of illustrious, yet of clever and talented, mothers. The stately poet of Weimar furnishes the most noticeable example of the genius and gifts of a mother descending to her son in increased and perfected ability. 'From my father,' Goethe writes, 'I inherit my frame and the steady guidance of my life; from dear little mother my happy disposition and love of story-telling.' And in Lewes's *Life of Goethe* the poet's mother is referred to as being 'one of the pleasantest figures in German literature, and one standing out with greater vividness than almost any other. She was the delight of children, the favourite of poets and princes. After a lengthened interview an enthusiastic traveller exclaimed, 'Now do I understand how Goethe has become the man he is.' The Duchess Amalia corresponded with her as an intimate friend; a letter from her was a small jubilee at the Weimar court.' The Italian poet, Torquato Tasso, is another instance of this form of hereditary genius ; and most of us have heard of the mother of England's greatest Greek scholar and verbal critic, Professor Porson,—the wonderful housemaid with the wonderful memory, whose master discovered that she had not only read all his books on the sly, but had a sound knowledge of all the books she had read.

The mother of Clough was a Yorkshire lady, the daughter of John Perfect, a banker at Pontefract, who was the son of another John Perfect, and grandson of a third ; the last-named being Mayor of Pontefract in 1737.[1] Her mother's maiden name was Catherine Maria Moseley. There seems to be little doubt that Clough's character and disposition were inherited from his mother, and were greatly influenced by her example and teaching. The following extract from a passage written by the poet's sister seems to prove very clearly that this was the case : it is taken from the memoir prefixed to 'The Poems and Prose Remains,' published in 1869 :—

[1] See Dr. Edward Miller's 'History and Antiquities of Doncaster and its Vicinity,' p. 393.

'My father,' she writes, 'was very lively, and fond of society and amusement. He liked life and change, and did not care much for reading. He had a high sense of honour, but was venturesome and over sanguine, and when once his mind was set on anything, he was not to be turned from it, nor was he given to counting consequences. My mother was very different. She cared little for general society, but had a few fast friends to whom she was strongly attached. In her tastes and habits she was rigidly simple; this harmonized with the stern integrity which was the foundation of her character. She was very fond of reading, especially works on religious subjects, poetry, and history; and she greatly enjoyed beautiful scenery, and visiting places which had any historical associations. She loved what was grand, noble, and enterprising, and was truly religious. She early taught us about God and duty, and having such a loving earthly father, it was not difficult to look up to a Heavenly one. She loved to dwell on all that was stern and noble. Leonidas at Thermopylæ, and Epaminondas accepting the lowliest offices and doing them as a duty to his country; the sufferings of the martyrs, and the struggles of the Protestants, were among her favourite subjects. There was an enthusiasm about her that took hold of us, and made us see vividly the things that she taught us. But with this love of the terrible and grand she was altogether a woman, clinging to and leaning on our father. When he left us, Arthur became her pet and her companion. I cannot but think that her love, her influence, and her teaching had much to do with forming his character.' . . . .

There is much in this that plainly indicates how closely the disposition of the poet resembled that of his mother. He, also, 'cared little for general society, but had a few fast friends to whom he was strongly attached.' He was 'fond of reading, especially works on religious subjects, poetry, and history ; and greatly enjoyed beautiful scenery.' He, too, 'loved to dwell on all that was stern and noble ; ' and of him it may be said, with especial fitness and truth, that he 'loved what was grand and enterprising, and was truly religious.' To one, therefore, who had only these facts before him, it would appear plain, and a matter respecting which there could be no manner of doubt, that the natural genius of Clough was inherited in its entirety from his mother. When we turn, however, to the genealogy of his father's family, given in Burke's *History of the Commoners*, vol. iii., p. 515, a new light is thrown upon the subject, and we at once discover that we have been too hasty in our surmises. The eye has but to pass a short distance up the lengthy genealogy before it meets with a somewhat startling discovery in the person of a Hugh Clough, who was born in the year 1746, and was Clough's father's uncle. He was a Fellow of King's College, Cambridge, and died at a very early age, yet not before he had shown indications of that poetic genius which was eventually to develop itself in the writings of his brother's grandson. He was a friend of the poet Cowper, and also of the poet William Hayley; and in the interesting *Memoirs* of the latter we find the following reference to his poetic talent, and early death :—' It was the lot of Hayley to lose and lament many of his early friends. One loss of this kind had already afflicted him. Among his private letters there is one addressed to a poetical youth of Wales, whose name was Clough, and whom he had left at Eton. Thence he (Clough) sent to the young poet of Sussex an elegant Latin *Ode to Venus*, and Hayley, in returning his thanks for so lively a present, concluded his letter with an

imitation in English verse of the ode he received ;
adding at the close of it some stanzas on the
country of his friend.' In a letter written by
Hayley to his mother some time afterwards, he
tells her how his feelings had been awakened and
sharply touched by the death of his friend Hugh
Clough, which had thrown a melancholy over his
nature.

Another interesting fact in the history of the
family is that one of the earliest members of it
given in the genealogy, whose name was Sir Richard
Clough, is said to have been related on his mother's
side to John Calvin. His father, who was also
named Richard, and who was commonly called
Hen, or the old, from having lived during the
reigns of Henry VII. and Henry VIII., of
Edward VI., and of the Queens Mary and Elizabeth,
married in the reign of Henry VIII., as recorded
in the *Harleian MSS.*, fol. 1971, and settled at
Lleweny Green, near Denbigh. It is not improbable
that he came from either Lancashire or Yorkshire,
as the name of Clough occurs in the ancient
charters of Whalley Abbey as early as the year
1315 ; and again in 1342 we find John del Clough,
a landowner in the same district, and owner of the

manor of Reved, situated on the borders of these two counties, granting land to be kept in trust for the Abbey. There is, moreover, a village of the name of Clough, in Yorkshire, not far from the town of Huddersfield. The word itself, too, appears to have been commonly used in the Northern counties to signify a cleft or ravine, or sometimes in a secondary sense to designate the stream or torrent flowing through it. Dr. Whittaker, in his famous *History of Whalley*, states:—'Clough, a narrow broken valley, is pure Saxon; but the etymologists have not observed that it comes from *cleofian*, *findere*, to cleave asunder. The Dutch *kloof* (from *kloven*) is the same word.' . . . . . And again, in another portion of the same work describing the country in the neighbourhood of Whalley, he writes :—' The rocky portion of Cliviger to the east abounds with waterfalls, some of which are of considerable depth and beauty. *Redwater Clough*, the course of the ancient Crow-brook, forms a bold and rocky boundary to the two counties. Here remains much native wood mingled with jutting points of crags, one large waterfall, and a small one of singular beauty near the top overshadowed by a single oak, which might

almost be painted of its own dimensions. On the
opposite side of the valley is *Beater Clough*, so
called probably on account of the 'beating' of the
waters. This contains a series of falls at least half
a mile in length. Next the west is *Ratand Clough*,
which retained the Saxon name of *Routand Clough*
(the 'brawling torrent') even in the time of Queen
Elizabeth.'

If, however, the word, or name, is of Saxon deri-
vation, as from the above would seem to be the
case, notwithstanding that Dr. Johnson states that it
is Norman, yet the district or county from which the
family originally came, must, we presume, remain
a matter of conjecture. We must, then, be content
to know that the Sir Richard Clough above referred to built the mansion of Plâs Clough, in the
county of Denbigh, about the year 1527, and that
the family have resided there ever since,—that is to
say, for more than three hundred and fifty years.
Of this Sir Richard it is recorded that he married
for his second wife, Katharine Tudor, heiress of
Berain and great grand-daughter of Henry VII.;
and the story is related that Sir Richard and
Morris Wynn of Gwydir accompanied her to her
first husband's funeral, and that Morris Wynn

when leading her out of the church after the service was concluded, requested the favour of her hand in marriage, to which she answered that she had already promised it as she went in to Sir Richard ; but that *should there be any other occasion she would remember him.* The story [1] is a good one, and the interest in it is enhanced by the fact that after Sir Richard's death she kept her promise to Morris Wynn and became his wife.

Sir Richard died at Antwerp in the year 1570, and his remains were interred there with the exception of the right hand and heart, which he desired might be transmitted to his native parish of Denbigh in a silver urn to be deposited on the coffin of the last possessor of his property. It should be mentioned that his second daughter, Catherine, became the wife of Roger Salusbury, and received from her father the house built by him and named Bachegraig, which afterwards came into the possession of the celebrated Mrs. Piozzi, her lineal descendant. But we are lingering too long among the musty rolls of old genealogies, and

[1] A full account of this anecdote will be found in Mr. Jenkinson's excellent ' Guide to North Wales.'

so without further delay we will turn at once to more recent times.

James Butler Clough, the father of the poet, was the third child in a family of ten children ; and, as it is generally the case in large families that some of its members have to seek their fortunes away from home, Clough's father had to leave the old house in Wales and to go into business as a cotton merchant at Liverpool. Here he resided several years, and here his four children, of whom Arthur was the third, were born. They were not destined, however, to remain at Liverpool for any great length of time, seeing that Arthur was but about four years old when his father removed with his family to Charleston, in South Carolina, U.S. At Liverpool they had been living little more than a day's march from the quiet neighbourhood of their ancestral home in North Wales,—from Plâs Clough and Lleweny Green : but now the great waves of the surging Atlantic were to roll between them and those whom they held most dear. Our human hearts bear a resemblance in some respects to the flowers and shrubs,—their roots penetrate into the ground where they grow,—their fibres fold themselves round the objects in their immediate

vicinity. As 'George Eliot' somewhere remarks,
'there is no sense of ease like the ease we feel
in those scenes where we were born, where
objects become dear to us before we have known
the labour of choice, and where the outer world
seems only an extension of our own personality,
which we accept and love as we accept our own
sense of existence and our own limbs.' Doubtless
it was not without pain that the poet's father and
mother embarked with their little ones on board
the vessel which was to carry them away to
America ;—and their new home at Charleston, a
'large, ugly, red-brick house near the sea,' as we
are told, must for a time, at least, have seemed
to them both strange and friendless. And yet
Charleston, even in those distant days (1823), was
not, by any means, a lonely or dull place, for it had
already 'gone into business,' and from the windows
of their home the children could see the large ships
anchored in its hospitable harbour. A modern
writer states that owing to the lowness of the
ground on which it is built the town presents a
peculiarly picturesque appearance, as its spires and
public buildings seem to rise out of the sea, while
the richness of the surrounding foliage gives the

place a particularly engaging aspect. The upper part of the city, at the time of which we write, was composed of pleasant villas adorned with verandahs, and in the gardens were planted almond and orange trees, and various scented flowering shrubs; in the streets, also, were planted trees which afforded no unwelcome protection from the burning rays of the Southern sun. In the summer, the poet's sister tells us, they went down to Sullivan's Island, where they lived in a sort of cottage built upon piles. Here were far-stretching, shell-sprinkled sands, the haunt of innumerable curlews, whose plaintive cries mingled with the weary monotone of the 'sea's listless chime.' Here, too, were beautiful groves of myrtle, and the place was altogether one well fitted to move the imagination in a thousand pleasant ways, stirring the fancies and sensibilities of boyhood, and furnishing memory with manifold vivid pictures of sunny scenes in a land where Nature had not as yet entirely relinquished the sceptre to culture and the arts of civilization. The country, perhaps, was scarcely to be described as 'stern and wild,' but it was none the less

'Meet nurse for a poetic child,'

and one can hardly doubt that long after his five
years' residence at Charleston had become a thing
of the past, golden visions of those sea-washed
sands, those groves of myrtle, and the lonesome
curlews with their piteous cry, visited from time to
time the youthful poet's memory, and were continually pictured in the bright and vivid mirror of
his imagination. The world in these days of his
childhood doubtless appeared to him to be sur-
passingly beautiful ; and perhaps to the poet this
must always, and under all conditions, however
unfavourable, be the chief characteristic of this
earth with its flowers and birds,—its smiling valleys
and uplifted peaks. There is a story told of
William Blake that one day a lovely child of
wealthy parents was brought to him as he sat in
his old worn clothes, amidst poverty, decent indeed,
but only one degree above absolute bareness : he
looked at her very kindly for a long while without
speaking, and then, gently stroking her head and
long bright curls, said, "May God make this world
to you, my child, as beautiful as it has been to
me!'

It was from the winter of 1822 to the summer of
1828, that is to say from Arthur's fourth to his

ninth year, that the family remained at Charleston ;
and during this early period of his life we are
told that he and his mother ' read much together,
histories, ancient and modern, stories of the Greek
heroes, parts of Pope's Odyssey and Iliad, and
much out of Walter Scott's novels.' No unfitting
foundation one must acknowledge for a poet's
literary education, and we say ' literary ' because
the poet's higher education must of necessity be
left to the later years of life, to the larger intelligence and more vigorous reason of manhood. The
higher education here referred to, it need hardly be
stated, is that which brings with it a knowledge of
Nature, and more especially of human-nature ;—
a clear perception of the realities of life as distinguished from its external and superficial aspects.
It is this higher education which raises such poets
as Shakspeare, Burns, and Wordsworth above the
heads of those who sing sweet songs of little
meaning, forgetting that if music alone were what
our hearts desired their tuneful piping cannot
yield us,

> ' to soothe our pains,
> Such multitude of heavenly strains
> As from the kings of sound are blown,
> Mozart, Beethoven, Mendelssohn.'

In the stories of the Greek heroes, in the Odyssey and Iliad of Homer, and in the novels by Sir Walter Scott, the young poet would find characters of rare nobility, brave hearts, and natures of Homeric grandeur and Homeric simplicity; and one cannot praise too highly the wisdom,—the rare and lofty judgment,—of a mother who could choose so well and so wisely the best intellectual nourishment for her favoured child.

There is a reference to these happy days at Charleston in one of the earliest (if not the earliest) of Clough's poems written in his boyhood when ill at Rugby, and while watching from his window Dr. Arnold's younger children at play. He writes:—

> ' I look'd upon thy children, and I thought of all
> and each,
> Of my brother and my sister, and our rambles on
> the beach,
> Of my mother's gentle voice, and my mother's
> beckoning hand,
> And all the tales she used to tell of the far, far
> English land.'

Soon, however, those 'rambles on the beach' were to come to an end, for in the summer of 1828 the Cloughs returned to England, and in the month of

October, instead of listening to the curlews in
South Carolina, Arthur found himself at school in
the quaint old town of Chester, the rest of the
family (with the exception of his eldest brother)
having sailed again to Charleston. In the following year he went to Rugby, and this brings us
to the first important stage of his life,—to the
point where he left the quiet bypaths of childhood,
and trod for the first time among jostling companions on the noisy highway of the world.

The influence of the spiritual atmosphere of Rugby
in moulding the character of Clough is so important
that we must here digress for a brief space with a
view to furnishing information to any that may be
unacquainted with the history of the school at this
period. In 1827, Dr. Arnold had been elected to the
post of Head Master, and it had been predicted at
the time by Dr. Hawkins that if Arnold was the
successful candidate he would change the face of
education throughout all the public schools in
England. That prediction has to a considerable
extent been verified, for the example set by Arnold
not only as a good schoolmaster, but as a good
man, has not been in vain. But what was the
character of him who has been called 'England's

greatest schoolmaster?' As a young man he is
thus depicted by John Keble, who was then a
curate at Hursley :—'Tom Arnold ran down here
like a good neighbour, and surveyed the premises
and the neighbourhood presently after Christmas.
How very unaltered he is, and how very comfortable and contented! He is one of the persons
whom it does one good to think of when I am in a
grumbling vein.'[1] Thus writes the genial author
of *The Christian Year*, the founder and origi-
nator of the High-Church, or Tractarian, movement, respecting one who may be almost said to
have been the founder of the opposite school,—
the Broad or liberal section of the Church. The
above description of Arnold, however, is naturally
incomplete, and a far clearer perception of his
character will be gained from the following excerpt
from the writings of a thoroughly competent
critic :—

'The basis of Arnold's *morale* reminds us of all
we know of that of another celebrated schoolmaster (not very popular in his day, and no great

---

[1] Keble afterwards found Arnold anything but 'good to
think of,' seeing that for years they were rather enemies
than friends.

favourite with such churchmen as Mr. Froude in later times), we mean John Milton. There is the same purity and directness about them both, the same predominance of the graver, not to say sterner elements, the same confidence, vehemence, and elevation. They both so lived in their 'great taskmaster's eye,' as to verify Bacon's observations in his *Essay on Atheism;* made themselves of kin to God in spirit, and raised their nature by means of a higher nature than their own. If men were as excitable by the example of the sublime in character as by the sublime in imagination, they would rise up from the contemplation of a certain greatness of soul, as Bouchardon the artist rose from Homer, when he rushed to the Comte de Caylus, his eyes on fire, declaring everybody he met seemed taller than before. Were we to stop here, what was formerly said of Cato would be equally true of Milton and of Arnold. Nobody could wish either of them *aut fortior, aut justior, aut temperantior,*—but *paulo ad lenitatem propensior,* very possibly.'

The main features of his character are plainly delineated in his letters, which are marked throughout by their extreme earnestness, and by their intolerance of all forms of wrong-thinking and wrong-doing. He loved what was pure and noble, and cherished lofty principles and large views. When seen from one side only he would appear stern and severe, and almost Puritanical in his abhorrence of the faults and evil tendencies of human nature; but from a different standpoint we behold him gentle, and loving, and truly affection- ate. Archbishop Whately writes respecting him that 'he was attached to his family as if he had no friends, to his friends as if he had no family, and to his country as if he had no friends or rela- tions.'

When Clough was removed from the school at Chester to Rugby, Arnold had been head master for little more than a year, but he had already impressed the stamp of his character upon the cus- toms and practice of the place, and more especially on the hearts and natures of those around him. In a notice written by the late Dean Stanley, in 1862, and which was published in the *Daily News* soon after Clough's death, we are told that, ' he (Clough) received into an unusually susceptible and eager mind the whole force of that electric shock which Arnold communicated to all his better pupils.

Over the career of none of his pupils did Arnold watch with a livelier interest or a more sanguine hope. By none, during those last years of school life, or first years of college life, was that interest more actively reciprocated in the tribute of enthu- siastic affection than by Clough.'

When we remember the very early age at which Clough went to Rugby,—he was only ten years old,—and when we also recall the fact that he remained there, gradually working his way from form to form, until he reached the top of the school and went to Oxford, it is hardly a matter of sur- prise that he should have become so thoroughly imbued, as he unquestionably did, with the especial qualities which are characteristic of the illustrious master at whose feet he sat. But in addition to this, there would appear to have been some inherent similarity in the natures and dispositions of the two men ; and it is not impossible that the pupil would, under any circumstances, and even if he had never known Dr. Arnold as a master or otherwise, have yet developed those particular virtues and modes of thought. This supposition is in a measure con- firmed by an observation made by Dean Stanley in the notice to which we have just referred : ' One trait,' he writes, ' which he shared with Arnold, but from an entirely independent and spontaneous source, and in a degree even more intense, was his sympathy with the sufferings and the claims of the poorer and humbler classes of the community.'

That such a pupil should have won the especial regard of such a master, is not to be wondered at ; still less that such a master should have won the enthusiastic affection of a boy like Clough, seeing that the loving admirers of the former were by no means limited to the members of his own household, but were to be found in unexpected and remote quarters.

On reading an interesting paper, published some thirty years ago, on the poems of Hartley Coleridge, we were astonished to meet with the following account of his admiration of Arnold :—

' That a character like that of Dr. Arnold, one which, though abounding in the kindly affections, was yet especially marked by its massive simplicity, its masculine energy, and its ever militant sense of duty, should have attracted the reverence of a man (Hartley Coleridge) so different, will be a matter of surprise to many. It was not, however, only in their love of wild flowers, and hatred of oppression and fraud, that they found a common ground. They shared the same great Christian convictions, and built on them their hopes for the human race. The same Faith which administered strength to the athlete cast upon the storms of active life, sustained the drooping spirits of the recluse.' . . .

'ON THE LATE DR. ARNOLD.

' Spirit of the dead !
Though the pure faith of Him that was on earth,
Thy subject and thy Lord, forbids a prayer—
Forbids me to invoke thee, as of yore
Weak souls that dared not meet their God alone
Sought countenance and kind companionship
Of some particular saint, whose knees had grazed
The very rock on which they knelt ; whose blood
Had made or sanctified the gushing well
Round which their fond, mistaken piety,
Had built a quaint confine of sculptured stone ;—
Yet may I hope that wheresoe'er he is—
Beneath the altar, by the great white throne,
In Abraham's bosom, or amid the deep
Of Godhead, blended with eternal light,
One ray may reach him from the humble heart
That thanks our God for all that he has been.
What he is now we know not : he will be
A beautiful likeness of the God that gave
Him work to do, which he did do so well.'

*   *   *   *

HARTLEY COLERIDGE.

It is probable that during the last two years of his life at Rugby Clough had the good fortune of seeing much of the society of Dr. Arnold, not only in school-hours, but also in the hours of recreation; for the latter had made it his practice to mix with, and closely cultivate the acquaintance of, the elder boys. This was a main feature of the system which he adopted for strengthening and confirming the discipline of the school, for he made use of the sixth form,—whose influence in controlling the younger boys is almost always capable of producing the most startling effects,—and by impressing upon them the importance of high principles of conduct, made them the bearers and teachers of his own views, not only for the time being, to the rest of the school, but afterwards to fresh companions at college and to the world at large. Hence we find Cardinal Newman when speaking of 'Liberalism' in his *Apologia Pro Vitâ Suâ*, p. 292, observes :—' The [Liberal] party grew all the time that I was in Oxford, even in numbers, certainly in breadth and definiteness of doctrine, and in power. And, what was a far higher consideration, by the accession of Dr. Arnold's pupils, it was invested with an elevation of character which claimed the

respect even of its opponents.' The two pupils whom
Cardinal Newman probably would have considered
especially representative of Dr. Arnold were doubtless the two friends at school and college, Arthur
Penrhyn Stanley and Arthur Hugh Clough,—the
two Arthurs whom Mr. Matthew Arnold has
immortalized in his exceedingly fine *In Memoriam*
poems of *Thyrsis* and *Westminster Abbey.*

As we have stated above, the intimacy between
Dr. Arnold and Clough was that of two kindred
natures, and in turning to the *Rugby Magazine*
for the years 1835 and 1836 we find many contributions by the latter, which bear traces of his illustrious
master's teaching. He was for some time the
editor of the periodical, which was in itself no small
honour when we remember the many other pupils
then at Rugby who have since distinguished themselves in various ways. The magazine is very interesting in that it contains many of his juvenile poems
which are not to be found elsewhere, and these
indicate what were the feelings and tendencies of
the boy-poet at this early age. We shall give one
or two extracts from these poems, at the same time
warning the reader that they are not to be taken
as fair specimens of the poet's style, but only as

showing the early development of the bud which
was eventually to grow into the perfect flower of
genius. It may, however, be mentioned, that if
compared with the juvenile poems of Byron, they
will be found to be unquestionably stronger, both in
thought and execution, and to be free from all the
doubtful sentimentalism of such lines as the following, which we quote from the second and third
poems given in the edition of Byron's works,
published by John Murray in 1857 :—

'TO E————.

'Let Folly smile, to view the names
   Of thee and me in friendship twined ;
Yet Virtue will have greater claims
   To love, than rank with vice combined.'

   *   *   *   *   *

'TO D————.

'In thee I fondly hoped to clasp
   A friend whom death alone could sever ;
Till envy, with malignant grasp,
   Detach'd thee from my breast for ever.'

   *   *   *   *   *

One cannot read such stanzas as these without
feeling a certain sense of pain, and yet there is in
them the germ of such beautiful lines as '*When we
two parted*,' and '*'Tis time this heart should be un-*

moved ;'—and so too in the following lines by Clough is the germ clearly traceable of the noble poems which he afterwards produced, of '*Say not the struggle nought availeth,*' and '*As ships, becalmed at eve that lay :'*—

'TO ——, ON GOING TO INDIA.

I.

' Come, brother, come away,
Already 'tis the hour of closing day,
Our wonted hour of converse sweet together,
Sweeter from memory of those sweet ones past
      In boyhood's sunny weather,—
Brother—dear brother—and is this the last ?

II.

' The west is waxing pale,
And the deep hollow of the hamlet dale
Is donning fast afar its misty shroud,
And from the covert of our old elm-tree
      The cuckoo calleth loud,
And for the last time, brother, unto thee !
      *   *   *   *   *

V.

'And now henceforward never
Will those stars look upon us both,—for ever
Lost unto us are Nature's sympathies :
On me thy sun and thy moon do not shine ;
      And other are thy skies ;
Yea ! ev'n thy heaven, my brother, is not mine !

VIII.

'Yet oh, when crushed and dead,
The sympathies of outward things have fled,
Remember that which lives and cannot die;
Ours may not be one home, nor ever will,
    Nor yet one land or sky,
But brother, brother, we have *one* God still.'

There is something in these stanzas that reminds
one of the calm sweetness, the placid grace, of Mr.
Matthew Arnold's poems *The Scholar-Gipsy* and
Thyrsis,—and especially of the lines

' Go, for they call you, shepherd, from the hill.
   *   *   *   *   *
Runs it not here, the track by Childsworth Farm,
Past the high wood, to where the elm-tree crowns
  The hill behind whose ridge the sunset flames?
  The signal elm, that looks on Ilsley Downs,
The Vale, the three lone weirs, the youthful Thames !—
   *   *   *   *   *

But these are the work of a poet's manhood; the
former were written by his friend when he was still
only a boy at school. It should be stated that
the above stanzas are not given in any of the
editions of Clough's poems, and have not, we
believe, been republished since they first appeared
in 1835 in the *Rugby Magazine*. This is also
the case as regards another poem entitled *The*

E

First of the Dead, in which the following lines
occur : —

'And thou art gone, my own dear one, the firstling of the
  grave,
And He hath taken lovingly, who bountifully gave :
       *   *   *   *   *
Joy's sunny day hath passed away, and Sorrow's night hath
  found us,
But the worlds that glaring lustre hid, are beaming now
  around us.
The beauty and the bliss of earth beguilingly they shone,
But the kingdoms of Infinity shine forth in night alone.'

It will be noticed that the thought contained in
these lines is similar to that set forth in Blanco
White's famous sonnet on 'Night and Death,' which
was republished in the *Gentleman's Magazine* in
the same year, it having previously appeared in
the *Bijou* for 1827. In another of Clough's juvenile
compositions a resemblance can be detected to
the versification of *Whistlecraft,* which Lord Byron
copied in his poems of *Beppo* and *Don Juan :*—we
quote one stanza as an example of the humorous
vein in Clough's character which disclosed itself
in the mirthfulness of some of his later poems,
and more especially in *The Bothie of Tober-na-
Vuolich.*

'Gentles that do, and gentles that do not
  Believe in ghosts, to what suits both I call you—
Ye that strong nerves, and ye that weak have got,
  Nor sentiment nor horror shall befall you ;
Ye that do shoot, and ye that never shot,
  To please you both I come with nought to gall you ;
O be ye sad or glad, or grave or gay,
Come, gentles all, come listen to my lay.'

   *   *   *   *   *

Probably a wise discretion has been exercised by the editors of the various editions of Clough's poems in omitting most of these early productions of the poet, for, indeed, the world would be no great loser if all the poems of all the poets written between the ages of twelve and sixteen were allowed to perish. The youthful editor of the *Rugby Magazine* seems, however, to have been unusually productive at this early period of his life, and this is the more surprising when we find that he had a taste for other and more boisterous pursuits. Thus Dean Stanley tells us, in the notice from which we have already quoted, that 'he did not, like some of the more distinguished of his contemporaries, hold aloof from the common world of schoolboy life with which *Tom Brown* has made us familiar, but mingled freely in the games and sports of his schoolfellows.' And another Rugbeian, Mr. Thomas Hughes, (the well-known author of *Tom Brown's School-days* and *Tom Brown at Oxford*) testifies to this account of Clough's character in an *In Memoriam* notice which appeared in the *Spectator* for November 23rd, 1861, very shortly after the poet's death ; and from which we give the following extract :—

' Arthur Hugh Clough was educated at Rugby, to which school he went very young, soon after Dr. Arnold had been elected head-master. He distinguished himself at once by gaining the only scholarship which existed at that time, and which was open to the whole school under the age of fourteen. Before he was sixteen he was at the head of the fifth form, and as that was the earliest age at which boys were then admitted into the sixth, had to wait for a year before coming under the personal tuition of the head-master. He came in the next (school) generation to Stanley and Vaughan, and gained a reputation, if possible, even greater than theirs. At the yearly speeches, in the last year of his residence, when the prizes are given away in the presence of the school and the friends who gather on such occasions, Arnold took the almost unexampled course of addressing him, and congratulating him on having gained every honour which Rugby could bestow, and having also already distinguished himself, and done the highest credit to his school, at the University. He had just gained a scholarship at Balliol, then, as now, the blue ribbon of undergraduates.

' At school, although before all things a student, he had thoroughly entered into the life of the place, and before he left had gained supreme influence with the boys. He was the leading contributor to the *Magazine;* and though a weakness in his ankles prevented him from taking a prominent part in the games of the place, he was known as the best goal-keeper on record, a reputation which no boy could have gained without promptness and courage. He was also one of the best swimmers in the school, his weakness of ankle being no drawback here, and in his last half passed the crucial test of that day, by swimming from Swift's (the bathing-place of the sixth) to the mill on the Leicester road and back again, between callings over.

' He went to reside at Oxford when the whole University was in a ferment. The struggle of Alma Mater to humble or cast out the most remarkable of her sons, was at its height. Ward had not yet been arraigned for his opinions, and was a Fellow and Tutor of Balliol, and Newman was in residence at Oriel, and incumbent of St. Mary's.'

It has been said by those who are entitled to speak *ex cathedrâ* on the subject, that the life of Clough was by no means an ' eventful ' life, and it is true that it does not include any great vicissitudes of fortune, any dreadful catastrophes, or any very perilous adventures. Yet if we take the word in the sense generally ascribed to it in the dictionaries, namely, as meaning *full of incidents or changes*, his life does to that extent appear to have been somewhat ' eventful.' For what are the rough outlines of his history, such as are usually given in the encyclopædias ?—

Born at Liverpool in 1819, he no sooner reached the age of four than he was called upon to make a voyage across the Atlantic,—in those days, at any rate, an incident or event of considerable interest ;— and the first nine years of his life not only witness a change from Liverpool to Charleston, from one continent to another, but also a visit to New York and other parts of America. At the age of nine he is brought back again to England, and after a year's

residence in the most antique town in the United
Kingdom, he is sent to be the pupil of the most
illustrious schoolmaster, and one of the most illustrious men of that period.　At the age of seventeen
he wins a scholarship at Balliol with a renown
beyond that of any of his predecessors.　'I remember, even to this day,' writes Dean Stanley,
'the reverberation of the profound sensation occasioned in the Common-room of that college,
already famous, when his youthful English essay
was read aloud to the assembled Fellows.　From
Balliol he was elected to a Fellowship at Oriel—a
distinction still at that time retaining something of
its original splendour.'　And the after-years of his
life—his presence at Oxford during the most eventful period of its history, his resignation of his Fellowship, his appointment to the post of Principal of
University Hall, London, his presence in Rome
during the time it was besieged by the French, his
residence at Cambridge, Massachusetts, and intercourse with Emerson, Longfellow, Lowell, and
other authors ; his appointment to the Education
Department, Whitehall, and afterwards as secretary
to a commission for examining the scientific military schools on the Continent ; his travels in the

South of France, the Pyrenees, Switzerland, and Italy, closing with his early death at Florence,—bring before our view a life full of incident, and full of change, and in that sense of the word may we not say an ' eventful ' life ?

Chapter II.

OXFORD.

THERE is an essay by the late Mr. Emerson in which he states that 'the great man, that is, the man most imbued with the spirit of the times, is the impressionable man,—of a fibre irritable and delicate, like iodine to light; who feels the infinitesimal attractions, whose mind is righter than others because it yields to a current so feeble as can be felt only by a needle delicately poised.' The wise and epigrammatic philosopher of Massachusetts is always instructive, and seldom conventional, and in the above excerpt from his writings, although we may doubt whether the 'impressionable man' is usually the man whose 'mind is righter than others,' one cannot fail to perceive the gem-like sparkle of a clear intellect. When Clough visited America in 1852, Emerson became his most intimate acquaintance, and these few words which we have here

quoted from the latter, seem especially applicable
to the former, and may be received as a succinct
and graphic description of the character of the
Oxford poet. Clough was emphatically an 'impressionable' man ; yet not, by any means, a man
'driven about by every wind of vain doctrine,' but
one quick to perceive and feel the least motion of
the spiritual atmosphere which surrounded him.
It is impossible for persons of this sensitive nature
to continue any length of time in one town or
country without becoming, to some extent, the
representative men of the place, and imbued in an
especial manner with the spirit that dominates
within its precincts. This is more especially the
case when the feelings of such persons, and their
natural intellectual tendencies, are in harmony with
those of the characters amongst whom they are
located, and when there is little that is repulsive or
uncongenial to be gulped down and assimilated as
best it may.

We are told that of all the scholars at Rugby
School, in the time when Arnold's influence was at
its height, there was none who so completely represented the place in all its phases as Clough.
And again when he had passed from school to

college, we find that he who had previously been a
representative Rugbeian, had now, after the expi-
ration of a very short period, become a typical
Oxonian ; and in a recently published history of
English literature we notice that he is referred to
as having been an 'Oxonian amongst Oxonians.'

His own writings, both in prose and verse, are
distinguished, in a marked manner, as showing
traces of the influence that a long residence at the
University had had upon the author.   This is
especially noticeable in the case of his *Long Vacation Pastoral, The Bothie of Tober-na-Vuolich*,
over which, as Mr. T. H. Ward observes, ' is thrown,
through the associations of the hexameter, a half-
burlesque veil of Academic illusion that produces
the happiest effect.'

Clough was, as we have said, an 'impressionable man,' but, it must be added, that he never for
any length of time lost the strong individuality
which so clearly distinguished him from the men
amongst whom he lived : and although he was, it is
true, emphatically an Oxonian, he was also, and
always, emphatically Clough,—the earnest and
subtle seeker after truth, the man whose nature
was marked by Homeric simplicity, and who,

while being one of the sceptics of the age, was, nevertheless, one of its most reverend, sincere, and devout spirits. Mr. Hutton, in his memoir of the late Walter Bagehot, writes as follows :—' It was of Clough, I believe, that Emerson was thinking (though knowing Clough intimately as he did, he was of course speaking mainly in joke) when he described the Oxford man of that day thus :—' Ah,' says my languid Oxford gentleman, 'nothing new, and nothing true, and no matter.' '

Although these words of Emerson did probably, as suggested, refer to Clough, yet we must protest very strongly against their being taken as being in any respect applicable to the poet, of all poets the most earnest and devout, who wrote those memorable lines :—

> ' It fortifies my soul to know
> That, though I perish, Truth is so :
> That, howsoe'er I stray and range,
> Whate'er I do, Thou dost not change.
> I steadier step when I recall
> That, if I slip, Thou dost not fall.'

It was in October, 1837, that Clough went into residence at Oxford, and it is necessary, in order to see clearly what were the influences now brought to bear upon his character, that some brief survey should be made of the state and condition, the dominant views and growing opinions, the spreading dissensions and party shibboleths, the spiritual contests, the excitement and angry warfare, the Liberalism and the Romanism, and all the tendencies and 'movements' of our leading University at that period.

Some twenty years, or more, before the date of the commencement of Clough's Oxford life, there had come up to the University as an undergraduate at Corpus Christi College, the son of a Gloucestershire clergyman, who was destined to become the inspiring genius of a small band of earnest men, the founders of an important religious movement. John Keble, for it is he to whom we refer, became a Fellow of Oriel at the very early age of nineteen, and remained a tutor at that college for five years. During this time he had been in the habit of writing 'religious poems in which devotional and domestic feelings were associated with habitual reverence for the ordinances of the Church.' He was not only a poet, but also Professor of Poetry at Oxford, and in the year 1827 (that is to say, exactly ten years before Clough's time), he published the volume of verse entitled the *Christian Year*, of which several hundred thousand copies are said to have been sold. Of this work very different estimates have been formed, but the general opinion is very much that expressed by Mr. J. A. Froude, in the following paragraph :—' The intellectual and literary quality of his work is, however, a fair subject of criticism ; and I am heretical enough to believe that, although the *Christian Year* will always hold a high place in religious poetry, it owes its extraordinary popularity to temporary and accidental causes.' But what is the account given of the book by one of its first and most illustrious admirers, by Keble's most able disciple, Cardinal Newman ?—' Much certainly,' he writes, 'came of the *Christian Year;* it was the most soothing, tranquillizing, subduing work of the day . . . Like the Shepherd's Pipe in the Oriental Vision, of which we are told, that 'the sound was exceedingly sweet, and wrought into a variety of tunes that were inexpressibly melodious, it was altogether different from anything I had ever heard. It put me in mind of those heavenly airs which are played to the departing souls of good men upon their first arrival in Paradise, to wear out the impressions of the last agonies, and to qualify them for the pleasures of that place.' . . . . Such was the gift of the author of the *Christian Year;* and he used it in attaching the minds of the rising generation to the Church of his predecessors, Ken and Herbert. *He did that for the Church of England which none but a poet could do ; he made it poetical* . . . . Poetry is the refuge of those who have not the Catholic Church to flee to, and repose upon . . . . her (the Catholic Church's) very being is poetry ; every psalm, every petition, every collect, every versicle, the cross, the mitre, the thurible, is a fulfilment of some dream of childhood, or aspiration of youth . . . . Keble's happy magic *made the Anglican Church seem what Catholicism was and is.* His poems became a sort of comment upon its formularies and ordinances, and almost elevated them into the dignity of a religious system.'

Of this paragraph there are two important sentences which we have italicized, for it is necessary to remember that in 1827 Keble made the Church of England poetical, and his magic made it seem what Catholicism really is. There is another reference to the author of the *Christian Year* which must be here quoted, and which occurs in Cardinal

Newman's chapter on 'Liberalism' towards the
end of the *Apologia;* it is as follows :—' But, as
far as I know, he who turned the tide, and brought
the talent of the University round to the side of the
old theology, and against what was familiarly called
March-of-mind, was Mr. Keble.   In and from
Keble the mental activity of Oxford took that
contrary direction which issued in what was
called *Tractarianism.'*

It was this Tractarianism, this 'movement'
endeavouring to make the Anglican Church seem
what Catholicism was and is, which was raging in
all its fulness at Oxford when Clough went into
residence.   'Since that time,' one may indeed say,
' Phaeton has got into the chariot of the sun ; we,
alas! can only look on, and watch him down the
steep of heaven.   Meanwhile, the lands which he
is passing over suffer from his driving.'

In the two years immediately following the
publication of the *Christian Year*, the political
world, and the religious world, had been agitated
by the repeal of the Test and Corporation Acts,
thus opening Parliament to dissenters, and by the
' Catholic Emancipation' in 1829.   In 1831, Lord
John Russell's Reform Bill was passed, and the

characteristic mark of the period was one of excitement, of change and progress, of general awakening, as though the generation that had grown to maturity with the newly-invented railways found the old institutions too slow for them, the old modes of life far too torpid for their quickened sensibilities. The 'slow coaches' were disappearing from the high-roads of the country, and the slow customs of our forefathers, with their weary dulness and lethargic dreariness, were no longer in keeping with the new age and were therefore doomed to disappear in due course. To quote Mr. M. Arnold's lines, which are not inapplicable to this period of our history :—

> 'Thundering and bursting
> In torrents, in waves—
> Carolling and shouting
> Over tombs, amid graves—
> See ! on the cumber'd plain,
> Clearing a stage,
> Scattering the past about,
> Comes the new age !
> Bards make new poems,
> Thinkers new schools,
> Statesmen new systems,
> Critics new rules !
> All things begin again ;
> Life is their prize ;

F

Earth with their deeds they fill,
Fill with their cries !'

Amongst the slow and superannuated customs of those days was the old style of long, dreary, Low Church services, in whitewashed buildings dedicated to the Holiness of Ugliness! The Rev. H. R. Haweis gives us an amusing, yet graphic description of them. He writes :—'What a dismal affair that 'old style' was! the parson in one box and the clerk in another, the parson nodding when the clerk was awake, and the clerk nodding when the parson was awake, and the congregation never awake at all, but dotted about in their high pews dozing through the ceremony, while half-a-dozen professional ladies and gentlemen in a gallery sang or did not sing, as it pleased them, but lolled about, fanning themselves, yawning or whispering, and generally showing the greatest contempt for the whole proceedings.'

The Low Church school was, indeed, a house ready to fall through its own weakness, and the Tractarian movement at Oxford, of which Keble, Dr. Pusey, and John Henry Newman were the triumvirate, would have done good work if they had contented themselves by introducing new life and light into our Church services, and by getting rid of the dreary dulness which soothed our ancestors into their peaceful sabbath-day slumbers.

Unfortunately this did *not* content them, nor was it, indeed, the chief object of their movement, but only a corollary, or contingency, of the system which they wished to introduce. The object at which they really aimed was to raise up and restore the ancient power of the Church with a view to resisting the Liberalism, and other revolutionary tendencies, which they conceived to have set in with the passing of the Reform Bill in 1831. Newman, who was the leader and instigator of the 'movement,' had by the perusal of the *Christian Year* been brought to believe that the ancient forms and institutions of the Church might be restored to their position of spiritual symbols, and that a Neo-Catholicism might take the place of Protestantism, which was too weak to resist the power of the new enemy.

In the spring of 1833 (that is to say, four years before the period of Clough's Oxford residence, to which we are gradually approaching) Newman and Hurrell Froude had been travelling in the south of Europe, and while at Rome had twice called upon

Monsignore (subsequently Cardinal) Wiseman at
the *Collegio Inglese.* Soon afterwards (as we are
told on the following page of the *Apologia*)
Newman began to think *that he had a mission,* and
when, on taking leave of Monsignore Wiseman, the
latter courteously, yet very prophetically, expressed
a wish that he might make another visit to Rome,
Newman replied (as he himself tells us) with great
gravity,—' *We have a work to do in England.*'
During the voyage back in an orange-boat bound
for Marseilles, he wrote the lines *Lead, kindly
light* ;[1] and on the Sunday after he reached
England Keble preached his famous sermon on
' National Apostacy,' which did much towards
spreading a zeal for the revival of religion among
the members of the University, and practically began
the religious movement of the Tractarian school.

Immediately after the delivery and publication
of this sermon by Keble, the 'Tracts for the
Times' were begun by Dr. Newman, as he tells us,

---

[1] He is by some persons reported to have composed these
lines on the night before he was converted to Roman Catholicism : this is a mistake, seeing that he remained a
member of the English Church for twelve years after they
were written.

'out of his own head.' It is right, however, that
we should mention that in the preceding year the
British Magazine, with the same views and the
same object as the Tracts, had been commenced by
Mr. Hugh Rose, who had been the first to call attention to the 'rocks ahead' of the Church of England;—
to the dangers arising from the biblical and theological speculations in Germany ;—and the far graver
perils, and threatened catastrophes, in the authori-
tative introduction of liberal opinions into this
country through the distribution of Church patronage
by the Whig Government. Dr. Newman, however,
goes a step further than Mr. Rose, for he writes :—
' Though the object of the movement was to with-
stand the Liberalism of the day, I found and felt
that this could not be done by mere negatives. It
was necessary for us to have a positive Church
theory erected on a definite basis. This took me
to the great Anglican divines ; and then, of course,
I found at once that it was impossible to form any
such theory, without cutting across the teaching of
the Church of Rome. *Thus came in the Roman
controversy.*'—[The Italics are employed to draw
the reader's attention to this important step in the
history of the Church of England's recent move-

ment towards Roman Catholicism.] The Tracts
were addressed, some of them, to the Clergy,
'Ad Clerum,' and some to the people, 'Ad
Populum;' and the first Tract which was issued,
and which was sold for a penny, was entitled
Thoughts on the Ministerial Commission, and
dwelt upon the Apostolical Succession of the
Bishops, and the sole priesthood of those whom
the Bishops ordained. The doctrine of the 'Apostolical Succession' would seem to be the missing
link between the Infallibility of the Pope of Rome
and the Protestantism of the English Church :
whether the 'Succession,' however, be complete
from an historical point of view, or not, we in England know, and if we are not forgetful of the truth
shall always be prepared to assert, that the 'Apostolical Succession' has been a succession of men
neither better nor worse than ourselves. It has
been truly recorded [1] that when the printing-press
was invented, and the Bible came to be read by the
people, the contrast was so violent between religion
as exhibited in the New Testament and religion as
taught and exercised by the 'Infallible Church'

[1] See Mr. Froude's 'Reminiscences of the High Church
Revival.'

that half Europe broke away from it. But if anyone still holds in the innocence of his, or her, heart
that the 'Apostolic Succession' is not only valid,
but of value as making the members of its lengthy
series either wiser, or more consistent in their
teaching, or purer in their manner of living, let him,
or her, go and study the history of Europe at the
time of the Reformation, or still better read carefully the writings of Luther and Erasmus.

The Tracts thus begun by Cardinal Newman
were the work of various persons who for the most
part agreed in their doctrine, but, as the founder of
the work points out, not always in the argu-
ments by which it was to be proved. The most
illustrious of the writers of them were, it need
hardly be stated, Keble and Pusey, but the list of
the persons more or less connected with the movement of which the Tracts were, so to speak, the main-
spring, includes Mr. W. E. Gladstone (the Premier
of England at the present time); Manning (now
Cardinal Manning); Frederick Faber, poet and
author of the beautiful hymn *The Pilgrims of the
Night;* Isaac Williams, of whom Mr. Froude
writes, 'He was a poet, too, and now and then
could rise into airy sweeps of really high imagina-

tion. There is an image in the *Baptistery* describing the relations between the actions of men here in this world and the eternity which lies before them, grander than the finest of Keble's, or even of Wordsworth's : '—

> ' Ice-chain'd in its headlong tract
> Have I seen a cataract,
> All throughout a wintry noon,
> Hanging in the silent moon ;
> All throughout a sunbright even,
> Like the sapphire gate of Heaven ;
> Spray and wave, and drippings frore,
> For a hundred feet and more
> Caught in air, there to remain
> Bound in winter's crystal chain.
> All above still silent sleeps,
> While in the transparent deeps,
> Far below the current creeps.
> Thus, methought, men's actions here,
> In their headlong fell career,
> Were passing into adamant ;
> Hopes and fears, love, hate, and want,
> And the thoughts, like shining spray,
> Which above their pathway play,
> Standing in the eye of day,
> In the changeless Heavenly noon,
> Things done here beneath the moon.'

These lines are clearly the work of an imaginative poet, who well deserves to rank with Keble, Newman, and Faber, as supplying the poetry which formed so important a factor in the Neo-Catholic enthusiastic advance.   Of the other Tractarians we may mention Hurrell Froude, Ward, Palmer, Percival, William Gresley, and the late Canon Oakeley.

The excitement occasioned by the movement was reaching its zenith when Clough arrived upon the scene of action at Oxford in 1837.   In the preceding year Monsignore Wiseman had come over from Rome (possibly to see how his two young Oxford friends were getting on with the 'work they had to do in England'), and had been delivering lectures in London on Catholicism, while Newman was just publishing his volume on 'The Prophetical Office of the Church viewed relatively to Romanism and popular Protestantism.'   (There is something curiously supercilious in the use of the term 'popular' as here applied ;—does it not somewhat suggest the words of the old Roman poet, *Odi profanum vulgus et arceo ?*)   At first Clough, as might be expected, was attracted by the poetry, the enthusiasm, the refinement, the zeal, the idealism, the devotion, and the various other virtues of the 'movement,' and for the first two years of his residence there seemed almost a possibility of his being carried away down

the stream flowing with so strong and swift a
current towards the Church of Rome. He himself
afterwards stated that he had been 'like a straw
drawn up the draught of a chimney,' but if this was
the case, we must, for our part, in all seriousness
add that he soon came out at the top, and once
more breathed the free, calm atmosphere of a
reasonable and liberal way of thinking. One of his
chief friends was the Tractarian Ward, and in a
letter written in his second term he states : 'I am
great friends with Brodie (afterwards Sir Benjamin
Brodie), and still more so, I think, with Ward,
whom I like very much.' And later in the same
year he writes : 'Among other incidents I have had
the pleasure of twice meeting the heresiarch
αὐτοτατος, namely, John Henry Newman, once at a
dinner-party, and once at a small and select breakfast. I was introduced, and had the honour of
drinking wine with him ; on the strength of all
which, of course, as is one's bounden duty, I must
turn Newmanist.' He had, however, other friends
and acquaintances of wider and wiser views, and
amongst these may be mentioned Dr. Richard Con-
greve (who is at the present time the leader of the
Positivist Religion in this country), the late Dean

Stanley, Professor Jowett (now master of Balliol College, Oxford), and Mr. Matthew Arnold. But it is hardly probable, even if this had not been the case, that his Tractarian friends would have long retained his sympathies, for the teaching of Dr. Arnold and his own natural intelligence rendered this almost impossible. While, ever and anon, like the sound of distant thunder, came some echoes of the angry chiding of the master of Rugby, as though the artillery of heaven was resounding over the heads of the Newmanite party. Thus, for instance, in a letter to A. P. Stanley, Dr. Arnold writes :—

'Now, with regard to the Newmanites, I do not call them bad men, nor would I deny their many good qualities ; . . . . I judge of them as I do commonly of mixed characters, when the noble and the base, the good and the bad, are strongly mixed up together. There is an ascending scale from the grossest personal selfishness, such as that of Cæsar or Napoleon, to party selfishness, such as that of Sylla, or fanatical selfishness, that is the idolatry of an idea or a principle, such as that of Robespierre and Dominic, and some of the Covenanters. In all these, except perhaps the first, we feel a sympathy more or less, because there is something of personal self-devotion and sincerity; but fanaticism is idolatry, and it has the moral evil of idolatry in it; that is, a fanatic worships something which is the creature of his own devices, and thus even his self-devotion in support of it is only an apparent self-sacrifice, for it is, in fact, making the parts of his nature or his mind, which he least values, offer sacrifice to that which he most values. I have been looking through the Tracts, which are to me a memorable proof of their idolatry; some of the idols are better than others, some being, indeed, as very a *Truncus ficulnus* as ever the most degraded superstition worshipped.'

There would possibly have been greater danger of Clough's finally adhering to the Neo-Catholic doctrines had he intended to devote himself to the priesthood, but that not being the case, even the persuasion of his friend Ward (who, if we remember rightly, became a pervert to Romanism a few months before Newman) failed to have any lasting effect upon his opinions; and it is interesting to note how affectionately and nobly Ward wrote respecting Clough after the latter's death. An instance of this is to be found in the following extract, which we quote from 'The Poems and

Prose Remains : '—' Certainly I hardly met anyone during my whole Oxford life to whom I was so strongly drawn. Among the many qualities which so greatly attracted me, were his unusual conscientiousness and high-mindedness and public spirit. . . . . The notion of preparing himself for success in a worldly career was so far from prominent in his mind, that he might, with some plausibility, have been accused of not thinking about it enough. But his one idea seemed always to be, that he should to-day do to-day's duty, and for the rest leave himself in God's hands. . . . . Then his singular sweetness of disposition : I doubt if I have anywhere seen this exceeded. I have known him under circumstances which must have given him great vexation and annoyance, but I never saw in him the faintest approach to loss of temper. . . . . He was never taken in with shams, pretences, and traditions, but saw at once below the surface.'

This is high praise ;—and it is precisely this last quality for which he is here eulogized, this power of *seeing below the surface of things*, that probably saved Clough from becoming a confirmed disciple of the Tractarian school. He had, moreover, an intense abhorrence of anything tending

to superstition, that upas-tree of which Shelley
wrote :—

> ' Thou taintest all thou look'st upon ! the stars
> Which on thy cradle beamed so brightly sweet,
> Were gods to the distempered playfulness
> Of thy untutored infancy ; the trees,
> The grass, the clouds, the mountains, and the sea
> All living things that walk, swim, creep, or fly,
> Were gods : the sun had homage, and the moon
> Her worshipper.'

But perhaps it will be said that the leaders of
the Tractarian movement cannot be charged with
any leaning, or tendency, towards superstition ;
and that this, therefore, could have had nothing to
do with Clough's staunch resistance to their influences. Yet let us look a moment and see what
account the author of the *Apologia* gives of himself and of Keble. At page 2 of that work he
writes :—' I was very superstitious, and for some
time previous to my conversion (when I was fifteen)
used constantly to cross myself on going into the
dark.' And again at page 28, where he refers to his
own opinions when he was just thirty years of age,
he states :—' It was, I suppose, to the Alexandrian
School and to the early Church, that I owe in particular what I definitely held about the Angels. . . .

I considered them (the Angels) as the real causes
of motion, light, and life, and of those elementary
principles of the physical universe, which, when
offered in their developments to our senses, suggest
to us the notion of cause and effect, and of what
are called the laws of nature. This doctrine I have
drawn out in my Sermon for Michaelmas day,
written in 1831.' The doctrine, in short, that
when the leafy branches of the aspen, or the acacia,
sway and bend before the wind, it is not the force
of the atmosphere, but the invisible hand of an
angel that is moving them! The doctrine that the
motion of the tides of the ocean is not really caused
by the influence of the sun and the moon, but by
angels that never weary of their everlasting labour,
and whose strength is equal to moving so vast a
body of water! This doctrine, which thus considers
' the Angels *to be the real causes of motion,*' may by
some persons be deemed an excellent illustration
of Professor Tyndall's definition of superstition as
being ' Religion which has grown incongruous with
intelligence.'

Of Dr. Keble he writes at page 290 :—'Keble was a
man who guided himself and formed his judgments,
not by processes of reason, by inquiry or by argument,

but, to use the word in a broad sense, by authority.
Conscience is an authority; the Bible is an authority;
such is the Church ; such is Antiquity ; such are the
words of the wise; such are hereditary lessons; such
are ethical truths ; such are historical memories,
such are legal saws and state maxims; such are proverbs ; such are sentiments, presages, and prepossessions.   It seemed to me as if he ever felt happier,
when he could speak or act under some such
primary or external sanction ; and could use argument mainly as a means of recommending or
explaining what had claims on his reception prior
to proof.   He even felt a tenderness, I think, in
spite of Bacon, for the idols of the tribe and the
den, of the market and the theatre.'

If this be a true picture of John Keble (and we
do not doubt the veracity of Cardinal Newman's
statements), then we have no hesitation in affirming
that it was morally impossible for Arthur Hugh
Clough to become his disciple.   Sentiments, presages, and prepossessions!   Antiquity, legal saws,
state maxims, and proverbs!   What a foundation
for the belief of the leader of a great religious
movement in this our nineteenth century!   We
can imagine Clough intimating that such finger-

posts as these usually point in the wrong direction, and that he who follows their guidance
may find himself in the enemy's camp. There is
an Italian 'proverb' which says, *Chi non sa niente,
non dubita de niente—He who knows nothing, doubts
of nothing :*—and one wonders whether this was
one of the finger-posts that Keble followed, or
whether he only read, and recognized those that
agreed with his own 'prepossessions.'—Possibly he
fell in with the 'maxim' which tells us that *All roads
lead to Rome !*—and so thought he might as well
choose the path which seemed the pleasantest, and
which, as we know, brought him very near to that
ancient city.

Then again as regards 'Antiquity,' which the
Tractarian party so firmly believed in, surely the
Vedas, and the teaching of Confucius, can scarcely
be considered modern ; and the writings of Lucretius are more ancient than those of St. Ignatius or
Basil :—why, then, urge the antiquity of the latter as
a reason for accepting their opinions if you reject
the former ? Astrology and witchcraft, augury and
divination, alchemy and trial by ordeal, fortune-
telling, felony, and bad roads (as Sydney Smith
would have said), these, or most of them, are as

ancient as the early Fathers, but they are not things to be admired or approved. Clough saw below the surface in this as in other matters, and in the following extract from one of his shorter poems we have the truth, crystallized and moulded into rhythmical shape, and stamped with the poet's own special mark of mingled reverence and intelligence.

> "'Old things need not be therefore true,'
> O brother men, nor yet the new ;
> Ah ! still awhile the old thought retain,
> And yet consider it again !
>
>   *   *   *   *   *
>
> Alas ! the great world goes its way,
> And takes its truth from each new day ;
> They do not quit, nor can retain,
> Far less consider it again.'

There is a letter by Dr. Arnold to 'C,' which may possibly have suggested these lines, a portion of which we think may be of interest to the reader ; and which we therefore venture to quote. It is as follows :—

'RUGBY,
'*April 5th*, 1837.

'I take this opportunity to answer your kind and interesting letter, for which I beg you to accept my best thanks. I can hardly answer it as I could wish, but I did not like to delay writing to you any

longer. . . . I am quite sure that it is a most solemn
duty to cultivate our understandings to the utter-
most, for I have seen the evil moral consequences
of fanaticism to a greater degree than I ever expected to see them realized ; and I am satisfied
that a neglected intellect is far oftener the cause of
mischief to a man, than a perverted or over-valued
one. Men retain their natural quickness and
cleverness, while their reason and judgment are
allowed to go to ruin, and thus they do work their
minds and gain influence, and are pleased at gaining it ; but it is the undisciplined mind which they
are exercising, instead of one wisely disciplined. . . .
Remember the words, ' Every scribe instructed to
the kingdom of God, is like unto a householder who
bringeth out of his treasure, things *new and old;* '
that is, who does not think that either the four
first centuries on the one hand, nor the nineteenth
century on the other, have a monopoly of truth.'

Although the followers of Newman (ὁ μέγας
Νέανδρος as Clough playfully called him) failed to
make a convert of the poet, the vortex of religious
excitement and discussion kept him idly moving in
its ceaseless gyrations, so that he had little time or

inclination for hard reading. 'I have,' he writes
in 1839, 'but little appetite for work, mathematical
or classical; and there is as little compulsion to it,
and as much enticement from it, as is possible in
our ways of life at Oxford.' The consequence of
all this was, as might well have been expected, that
Clough failed to obtain a first class in the schools,
much to the surprise and disappointment of his
friends, especially of Dr. Arnold. Yet there is
little doubt that occasionally, at any rate, Clough
did read hard, for we hear of his passing a whole
winter in his rooms at Balliol without a fire—an
excellent method, he said, of keeping out visitors, as
nobody else could stand the cold for more than a
few minutes. We notice that in the memoir prefixed to his works it is said that his rooms *were on
the ground floor*, while Mr. A. Lang in a recent
article on Mr. Matthew Arnold tells us, that when he
(Mr. Lang) was an undergraduate at Balliol fifteen
years ago, 'the rooms which Clough was said to
have occupied were shown to the inquiring fresh-
men; and that they were *quaint and tiny garrets in
the roof of the old quadrangle* which has since been
pulled down, and has been replaced by the present
amazing structure, so much more remarkable for

point than for feeling.' This reminds one of the story of the unfortunate genealogist who discovered that he had unhappily been weeping over the wrong grave! But in Clough's case the probability is, that during his residence at Balliol he removed from one set of rooms to another; and hence this apparent discrepancy between Mr. Lang's account and that given in the memoir.

This power of enduring cold appears to have been characteristic of the poet, for he is said to have bathed every morning, through the whole of one winter, in the cold Holywell baths. We remember that in our own undergraduate days (now, alas! some seventeen years ago) we used occasionally to go before morning chapel to bathe at Parson's Pleasure in the month of March, when the grass was still white with the hoar-frost, and we can therefore to some extent appreciate what must have been the feelings and endurance of one who was not to be intimidated by the snow and ice of January or December. Of all the out-door enjoyments of life that of bathing was the one which Clough loved best, and for a good swimmer there is probably no other exercise so invigorating and delightful.

The following lines by Professor Shairp are taken from a poem entitled *Balliol Scholars: A Remembrance*, published in 1873. They contain one of the most striking and graphic pictures of Clough, as he appeared to his brother Oxonians, that we remember to have met with, and refer in passing to the contending influences upon his character of John Henry Newman's preaching at St. Mary's, and the early teaching of Dr. Arnold.

*　　　*　　　*　　　*

'Foremost one stood, with forehead high and broad,—
　Sculptor ne'er moulded grander dome of thought,—
Beneath it, eyes dark-lustred rolled and glowed,
　Deep wells of feeling where the full soul wrought ;
Yet lithe of limb, and strong as shepherd boy,
He roamed the wastes and drank the mountain joy,
　To cool a heart too cruelly distraught.

'The voice that from St. Mary's thrilled the hour,
　He could not choose but let it in, though loath ;
Yet a far other voice with earlier power
　Had touched his soul and won his first heart-troth,
In school-days heard, not far from Avon's stream :
Anon there dawned on him a wilder dream,
　Opening strange tracts of thought remote from both.

'All travail pangs of thought too soon he knew,
　All currents felt, that shake these anxious years,
Striving to walk to tender conscience true,
　And bear his load alone, nor vex his peers.

From these, alas ! too soon he moved apart ;
Sorrowing they saw him go, with loyal heart,
  Such heart as greatly loves, but more reveres.

' Away o'er Highland Bens and glens, away
  He roamed, rejoicing without let or bound,
And, yearning still to vast America,
  A simpler life, more freedom, sought, not found.
Now the world listens to his lone soul-songs ;
But he, for all its miseries and wrongs
  Sad no more, sleeps beneath Italian ground.'

      *   *   *   *

Chapter III.

OXFORD *(Continued)*.

THE Tractarian movement (as stated in the preceding chapter) failed to make a convert of Clough,—but it is said, by those who had the best opportunity of forming an opinion, that the discussion and questioning, the continued pondering on religious problems, occasioned by the Oxford revival, had the ultimate effect of driving him far away into the misty land of Doubt and Uncertainty. His views respecting the fundamental points of religious belief were dimmed and disturbed; and this excitement respecting the ordinances, ceremonies, and traditions of the Church, left him only wearied and dissatisfied,—

> ' Wandering between two worlds, one dead,
> The other powerless to be born.'

The late Dean of Westminster, in the paper from which we have already quoted two extracts, writes :

' Beyond his Oxford days I will not follow him.
It was his misfortune that those Oxford days were
cast in the time of that great theological tempest,
which (as Professor Goldwin Smith well remarks
in his *Lectures on Modern History*) has cast the
wrecks of the most gifted minds of the University
on every shore. This is not the place to inquire
into the precise nature of his religious views then
or afterwards. But whoever will be most inclined
to condemn his opinions in after years may be
assured that a vigorous analysis of the process
by which he arrived at them will trace them, in
great measure, to an abrupt and excessive reaction
against the school of theology then dominant in
Oxford, by which he was not only influenced, but
for a time fascinated and subdued. When at last
he broke away from the University and the Church,
it was with the delight of one who had known
more than other men the weight of the yoke which
ecclesiastical authority had once laid upon him.
The effects of this conflict were never entirely
effaced. The reserve which marked, I believe, all
his communications on these subjects, not less than
the opinions themselves which he entertained, was
a direct result of the vehemence of the struggle

through which he had passed ; and to this must in
part be attributed the torso-like state in which his
life is now left to us.   Those who knew him well
know that in him a genius and a character of no
common order has passed away, but they will
scarcely be able to justify their knowledge to a
doubting world.'

Mr. Hughes, also, writes to the same effect
respecting this period of the poet's life, and the
results which followed, so far as Clough was concerned, from the Newmanistic revival of Catholicism
at Oxford. 'Clough's was a mind,' he writes, ' which,
under any circumstances, would have thrown itself
into the deepest speculative thought of its time.
He seems soon to have passed through the mere
ecclesiastical debatings to the deep questions
which lay below them.   There was one lesson—probably one only—which he had never been able to
learn from his great master, namely, to acknowledge
that there are problems which intellectually are not
to be solved by man, and before these to sit down
quietly.   Whether it were for the harass of thought
on such matters which interfered with his regular
work, or from one of those strange miscarriages in
the most perfect of examining machines, which

every now and then deprives the best men of the highest honours, to the surprise of every one Clough missed his first class. But he completely retrieved this academical mishap shortly afterwards by gaining an Oriel fellowship. In his new college, the college of Pusey, Newman, Keble, Marriott, Wilberforce, presided over by Dr. Hawkins, and in which the influence of Whately, Davidson, and Arnold had scarcely yet died out, he found himself in the very centre and eye of the battle. His own convictions were by this time leading him far away from both sides in the Oxford contest ; he, however, accepted a tutorship at the college, and all who had the privilege of attending them will long remember his lectures on logic and ethics. His fault (besides a shy and reserved manner) was that he was much too long-suffering to youthful philosophic coxcombry, and would rather encourage it by his gentle 'Ah! you think so,' or, 'Yes, but might not such and such be the case ?'' Another of Clough's friends, the late Mr. Walter Bagehot, takes however a very different view of this gently questioning habit of the poet, for he observes, in his *Literary Essays*, 'Several survivors may think they owe much to Mr. Clough's quiet question, 'Ah, then, you

think ——?' Many pretending creeds and many
wonderful demonstrations, passed away before that
calm inquiry. He had a habit of putting your own
doctrine concisely before you, so that you might
see what it came to, and that you did not like it.'

Another writer—the present Dean of St. Paul's
—(who tells us that though knowing Clough but
slightly he nevertheless watched with a deep
interest the stormy and chequered career of the
poet) makes the following observations respecting
the change which took place in Clough's religious
views between the year 1841, when he took his
B.A. degree, and 1848, when he resigned his
Fellowship :—

'We have before us the spectacle of a mind of
singular conscientiousness, purity, and philan-
thropy, which was subjected to the influence of
two great waves of thought, Arnoldism and Tractarianism ; and which, after being sensibly affected
by both, deserted both for a vague scepticism.
Many are, no doubt, prepared to condemn, with
equal severity, each of these schools, and to look
upon such an issue as occurred in Clough's case as
the natural result of such training.'

But here we would point out, with reference to

the 'vague scepticism' to which Dean Church
refers, that those lines by Mr. Tennyson, which are
so full of the liberal and large-minded views of the
Poet-Laureate's earlier compositions, are especially
applicable to Clough's state of uncertainty,—we
mean the lines,

> ' There lives more faith in honest doubt,
> Believe me, than in half the creeds.'

There are many and various forms of Faith—or of
what commonly passes for such—to be found in
England at the present time, but one has little
hesitation in stating that a form, by no means rare,
is that of the man who is so much occupied with
the world about him, with the demands of society,
of pleasure and business, that he has not even time
to inquire what are the foundations of his belief.
He heedeth not the precept of St. Peter, ' Be ready
always to give an answer to every one that asketh
you a reason of the hope that is in you : '—and the
words addressed to the woman of Samaria, ' Ye
worship ye know not what,' are the very words
which seem most applicable to such ' light half
believers of our casual creeds.' ' What is truth ? '
said jesting Pilate, and would not stay for an

answer! but there are many amongst us who have
never advanced so far as that, and to whom it has
never occurred to make any such inquiry.

Clough was not a believer of this description,
since the lines in which Mr. M. Arnold refers to
himself are also true of Clough—we mean the lines
which occur in the 'Stanzas from the Grande
Chartreuse,'—

> ' For rigorous teachers seized my youth,
> And purged its faith, and trimm'd its fire,
> Shew'd me the high white star of Truth,
> There bade me gaze, and there aspire.'

It was the poet's aspiration after Truth, his eager
desire to follow the teaching of the Bible, *that
every man be able to give a reason of the hope that
is in him*, that was the cause of his hesitation
in accepting as the creed of his manhood either this
or that dogmatic form of Christianity. If we
turn to 'The Poems and Prose Remains,' vol. i.,
p. 111, we find in a letter written in 1847 a
paragraph which indicates very plainly what was
the poet's position at that time ;—he is speaking
of the 'Atonement,' and writes:—' The Evangeli-
cals gabble at it, as the Papists do their Ave Marys,
and yet say they know ; while Newman falls down

and worships *because* he does not know, and knows
he does not know. I think others are more right,
who say boldly, we don't understand it, and therefore we won't fall down and worship it. Though
there is no occasion for adding, 'there *is* nothing in
it;' I should say, until I know, I will wait, and if
I am not born with the power to discover, I will do
what I can with what knowledge I have—trust to
God's justice, and neither pretend to know,
nor without knowing pretend to embrace, nor yet
oppose those who, by whatever means, are increasing or trying to increase knowledge.'

It is just thirty-five years since that letter was
written, and we know how greatly the views,—the
orthodox views,—respecting the doctrine of the
Atonement, have changed during those years. We
can remember, at a period subsequent to the date
of this letter, being taught both at Church and
school that Christ suffered upon the Cross *to appease
a Father's anger;*—and now we presume, that if a man
were to utter a doctrine so crudely anthropomorphic
he would almost be counted as a blasphemer. Afterwards we remember being taught that Man having
sinned, Justice required *so much suffering as would
atone for that sin,*—a doctrine hardly better than the

former—for Justice would not be satisfied unless the person who committed the sin also bore the suffering. The truth is—*tempora mutantur et nos mutamur in illis*—the times are changed, and our opinions have changed with them ;—while the ortho-doxy of one age becomes the blasphemy of the next.

We are, however, inclined to think that Clough has been credited with a far larger amount of heterodoxy than he is properly entitled to, for when we turn to the current literature of the day, to our *Westminster*, *Fortnightly* and *Contem-porary Reviews*, to the *Spectator*, the *Nineteenth Century* or the *Times*, we cannot but think that for the most part they are quite as 'advanced' in their views as was the author of *Dipsychus :*—much as we admire his writings, we do not wish him to be credited with more than his due share of any quality, whether commendable or otherwise. Pos-sibly at the time in which he lived his opinions were not so general as they have since become,—possibly it is true that swimming, fearless and fore-most, down the currents of the spiritual river, he cried out to his lagging contemporaries to come on, —but now for nearly a quarter of a century he has lain buried on the banks of the stream of life, and his once too tardy companions have floated onwards and left him behind. Of dogmatism, and uncharitable intolerance of other people's tenets and beliefs, he was as free as it is possible for a person to be without parting with that one dogmatism which teaches the necessity of goodness and truth. Intolerance was a thing for which he had no sympathy. 'Intolerance,' he writes in a letter to Mr. Tom Arnold,—'intolerance, Tom, is not confined to the cloisters of Oxford, or the pews of the Establishment, but comes up, like the tender herb, *partout*, and is indeed in a manner indigenous in the heart of the family-man of the middle classes.'

It was in 1841 that Clough took his degree, and in the following year he was elected a Fellow of Oriel, and afterwards appointed Tutor of that College. He accordingly continued to reside at the University up to the time when he resigned both his Tutorship and Fellowship in 1848. The life of an Oxford don would seem by no means an unpleasant life. It possesses a sufficiency of employment to avoid the tedium of idleness, and a sufficiency of idleness to prevent anyone from being overworked. It is pleasantly varied by the continued interchange of term-time and vacation, and while the former is passed among congenial spirits at the University, the latter affords ample opportunity for whatever rambles may seem desirable,—for visits to Greece, Germany, or Norway,—for climbing the Matterhorn, or the equally terrible Schreckhorn,—for a voyage to the Faroe Islands, or whatever else may best suit the taste of the wanderer.

Clough is said to have proved an excellent tutor, and to have been exceedingly beloved by the undergraduates. Like Dr. Arnold, he appears to have delighted in taking long 'constitutionals' across country, and there are few towns that can vie with Oxford as regards the number of pleasant walks to be found in its immediate vicinity. To some of these Dr. Arnold refers in the following extract from a letter written to Clough soon after the latter went to the University :—' I cannot think that you are yet thoroughly acquainted with the country about Oxford, as you prefer the Rugby fields to it. Not to mention Bagley Wood, do you know the little valleys that debouch on the Valley of the Thames behind the Hinkseys ; do you know Horspath, nestling under Shotover ; or Elsfield, on its green slope, or all the variety of Cumnor Hill ;

or the wider skirmishing ground by Beckley,
Staunton St. John's, and Forest-hill, which we
used to expatiate over on whole holidays?' Possibly at the time he received that letter he did not
know all these choice places of the picturesque
country around Oxford, but that he did eventually do so we gather from the *In Memoriam*
poem in which his friend and brother poet Mr.
Matthew Arnold has immortalized his memory
under the name of *Thyrsis* and of which the following is the first stanza :—

'How changed is here each spot man makes or fills !
   In the two Hinkseys nothing keeps the same ;
The village-street its haunted mansion lacks,
   And from the sign is gone Sibylla's name,
And from the roofs the twisted chimney-stacks :—
   Are ye too changed, ye hills ?
See, 'tis no foot of unfamiliar men
   To-night from Oxford up your pathway strays !
   Here came I often, often, in old days ;
Thyrsis and I ; we still had Thyrsis then.'

*   *   *   *

And again, in other verses of the poem, we read :—

'Thou too, O Thyrsis, on like quest was bound !
   *   *   *   *
And this rude Cumner ground

Its fir-topped Hurst, its farms, its quiet fields,
  Here cam'st thou in thy jocund youthful time,
  Here was thine height of strength, thy golden prime ;
And still the haunt beloved a virtue yields.

       *   *   *   *

' Too rare, too rare, grow now my visits here !
  But once I knew each field, each flower, each stick ;
And with the country-folk acquaintance made
  By barn in threshing-time, by new-built rick.
Here, too, our shepherd-pipes we first assay'd.
  Ah me ! this many a year
My pipe is lost, my shepherd's holiday !
  Needs must I lose them, needs with heavy heart
  Into the world and wave of men depart ;
But Thyrsis of his own will went away.

' It irk'd him to be here, he could not rest !
  He loved each simple joy the country yields,
    He loved his mates ; but yet he could not keep,
  For that a shadow lower'd on the fields,
    Here with the shepherds and the silly sheep !
      Some life of men unblest
He knew, which made him droop, and fill'd his head.
  He went ; his piping took a troubled sound
  Of storms that rage outside our happy ground ;
He could not wait their passing.' * * * *

But it was not with walks about Oxford only
that Thyrsis satisfied his longing for the delight
imparted by Nature,—by gleaming landscapes and
sunny pathways, by wanderings in the sweet spring

days amid 'whitening hedges and uncrumpling fern.' His soul occasionally, at any rate, took an ampler sweep, for in one of his letters he writes :— 'I had a delightful walk to Braunston and Rugby, and still more so back here—about fifty miles, and mostly through fields and green lanes—quite a new way, and far pleasanter than the old one.' This reminds one of Porson, who, we are told, used sometimes to walk from Cambridge to London in order to dine at his club in the evening, the distance being *more than fifty miles*. A walk before dinner is no doubt a good thing, but there is no need to make it unnecessarily long ! Pedestrian feats such as these quite throw into the shade the lengthy perambulations of the poet Wordsworth, who on wintry days would plod all the way from Rydal to Keswick, 'on his indefatigable legs' (as Professor Dowden tells us), in order to take tea with Southey at Greta Hall.

But as regards Porson it would seem as though his dinners sometimes made his memory (that wonderful memory !) more remarkable than his presence of mind, for it is related that on one occasion when a friend meeting him in the street politely invited Porson to come and dine with him,

Porson bowed and replied, ' Thank you, sir, I dined yesterday ! '

Of Clough's other amusements at this period may be mentioned that afforded by a debating society to which he belonged, named the *Decade*, and of which the following account has been given by Dean Church (who appears to have himself been a member of it) in the *Christian Remembrancer* for January, 1863 :—' About 1840, if we are not mistaken, there was formed a small society for discussion, which, from its being originally limited to ten members, was called the *Decade*. It was afterwards enlarged, and one (if not more) of those admitted, when he looked round on those by whom he sat, might well feel with Ivanhoe that he ' was a young knight of lesser renown and lower rank, assumed into that honourable company, less to aid their enterprise, than to make up their number.' Considering, however, that the *Decade* did not last above ten or twelve years, and that the entire number of its members from first to last was probably under thirty, a fair share of influence and celebrity has certainly fallen to the lot of those who composed it.[1] Two won for themselves an

[1] Two *jeux de mots* in connection with the society may

honourable place in the House of Commons, one is
the eminently successful governor of a far-away
colony, one became head of an English theological
college, several have been tutors of leading colleges
in Oxford, four are at this moment professors in
that University, and professors (we may add) who
have made themselves felt far beyond the usual
circle of academic influences.   Considered as a
training-school for public speaking, the *Decade*
was decidedly inferior to the general debating
society known as the *Union*.   But the smaller
assembly had the advantage of being able to
handle more recondite subjects than would have

possibly amuse the reader. On the occasion of one of its
earliest meetings, a scout rushed into the rooms of a member
of Exeter College, saying that a gentleman was on the stair-
case who wanted to know where would be the meeting of the
Decayed for that evening.   The person applied to playfully
remarked to a friend that this misplaced accentuation augured
ill for the permanence of the society.   Another member of
the last-named college, who was disappointed at the kind of
discussions carried on at the society's meetings, said that had
he known how dull it was—

πολλαί κεν δεκάδες δενοίατο οἰνοχόοιο ;

the felicity of this application of Agamemnon's speech lying
in the circumstance that the concluding word was a translation of the speaker's name.

been suitable for the atmosphere of the more numerous one; and its members enjoyed the advantage of listening to several rising men who never addressed the *Union*. Here, as elsewhere, there needed something to break through Clough's natural shyness and reserve of manner. But occasions did arise when these impediments to the development and display of his fine powers were scattered to the winds; and at such times it was the opinion of some who were no mean judges, that in that brilliant *coterie* he fairly proved his right to the very first and highest place.

'We do not pretend to have enjoyed many opportunities of hearing Clough speak; but we did hear enough to make us believe that the above verdict was not far from the truth. Two great manifestations of his loftiness of tone and force of argument we can more especially call to mind; and after the lapse of more than sixteen years there can, we trust, be no indecorum in dwelling upon them for a few moments.

'One of these discussions arose out of a motion to the effect 'that Alfred Tennyson is the greatest English poet of the age.' This was brought forward by a gentleman of elegant and highly cul-

tivated taste, whose growing influence in parliament
and in the press was destined to be cut short by
death at a still earlier period of life than was
allotted to Clough. It had, we believe, been expected that a counter-claim on behalf of William
Wordsworth would be urged by a member bearing
a name associated with the Lake Country, as well
as with Rugby, and who has since proved a special
right to have an opinion on such matters. But
owing to the accidental absence of this gentleman,
the task was undertaken by Clough. It would not
be fair to record Clough's judgments upon the
present Laureate, nor the grounds on which he
avowed his preference for Mr. Tennyson's prede-
cessor, especially when we consider that neither
In Memoriam nor the *Idylls of the King* had
as yet been published. But the address he then
made was in every respect well calculated to
establish the truth of all that his intimate friends
maintained concerning him. It was characteristic
of the speaker, that just after his opening sentences,
he observed the entrance of two or three who had
arrived too late for the speech of the mover. 'For
the benefit of those members who have just joined
us,' said Clough, ' I will briefly recapitulate the case

that has been alleged on behalf of Tennyson.' He
then proceeded, with much terseness and admirable
fairness, to give a short summary of the speech of
his gifted opponent.'

Discussions respecting the comparative greatness
of poets are interesting and amusing, but are otherwise of very little value, for it is plainly idle to
say either that Tennyson is a greater poet than
Wordsworth, or Wordsworth than Tennyson, since
each is our greatest poet in his own particular line.
We have most of us, however, heard of the famous
debate at the *Union* as to whether Shelley or
Byron was the greater poet ;—it occurred about the
same time as the one at the *Decade* referred to
above, and has been described by no fewer than
three illustrious authors,—by Cardinal Manning,
Lord Houghton, and Sir F. H. Doyle,—all of
whom spoke on the memorable occasion. A Mr.
Sunderland and Arthur Hallam (whose 'deathless
praises' have been sung by Mr. Tennyson in *In
Memoriam*) also took part in the debate. Sir
Francis Doyle writes :—' Lord Houghton has pic-
turesquely introduced Mr. Gladstone, who really
had very little to do with the business, except that
he came afterwards to supper—a feat that might

have been accomplished with equal success by a man of much inferior genius.' Cardinal—in those days Mr.—Manning, of Balliol, spoke last, and to this effect:—We have all read Byron, and if Shelley had been a great poet, we should have read him also; but we have not done so; *ergo*, Shelley is not so great a poet as Byron. '*In hanc sententiam*'—the mover of the debate adds—'an immense majority of the *Union* went *pedibus*: the debate was over, and we all of us, *including Mr. Gladstone*, adjourned to supper.'

But to return to the *Decade*. Dean Church writes that on the other occasion when he heard Clough speak, 'a motion was proposed to the effect that the State ought to make some formal recognition of the growing power of the manufacturing interest. This gave an opening for the expression of some of the poet's strongest and most vehement convictions. In a speech which electrified some even of those among his audience who were by no means ultra-Conservative, he gave vent to his feelings about the claims of the poor, the duties incumbent upon holders of property, and such like topics. Our recollections of Clough's attitude in this debate enable us thoroughly to understand

and appreciate the following portion of Canon
Stanley's letter :—' One trait which he shared with
Arnold, but from an entirely independent and
spontaneous source, and in a degree even more
intense, was his sympathy with the sufferings and
the claims of the poorer and humbler classes of the
community. This, at one period, may have led
him into an excessive regard for the more democratic and socialist tendencies of opinion, both here
and in France. Many letters, partly playful, partly
serious, exist, describing with truly dramatic power,
and at the same time generous enthusiasm, his
impressions of Paris in 1848, and of Rome in 1849.
But this, or at least the outward expression of this,
passed away, under the disappointment, which I
believe that he felt (something akin to that of the
Reformers of the last century), on the futile issue of
that year of blasted revolutions. Still the feeling
itself was permanent, and one which, even to those
who could not enter into it, was touching and
edifying in the highest degree. A record of it
remains in a striking pamphlet (now probably very
scarce) which he published at Oxford, on the Irish
famine in 1847, in which (to use his own words)
" the graces and splendours of composition were

thoughts far less present to his mind than Irish
poor men's miseries, English poor men's hardships,
and (addressing himself to the youth of Oxford)
your unthinking indifference. Shocking enough
the first and the second, almost more shocking the
third. . . . . There is one thing about which you
must not do as you please. You must not insult
God and man alike with the spectacle of your
sublime indifference. The angels of heaven, one
might believe, as they pass above those devoted
shores, in gazing on that ordained destruction let
fall untasted from their immortal lips the morsel of
ambrosial sustenance. If we, as they, were nurtured
on other food than our brothers, if no gift of ours
could allay those pangs of famine, still methinks
this undisturbed, unrestrained fruition were not
wholly free of guilt. How much more, when every
crumb we touch is abstracted from that common
stock, which, in the Eternal registers is set down,
I fear, as scarcely less theirs than ours.'

'The great lesson which Clough seemed anxious,
in his speech as in the above pamphlet, to impress
upon others, was, that (to use his own words so far
as we can remember them) the possession of wealth,
or station, was a call, not to self-indulgence, but to

self-denial. And if this teaching was combined
with an amount of socialism with which we are
unable to sympathize, it must be borne in mind
that there was little peril in that direction to be
apprehended among those whom he addressed.
The temptation both among academic authorities
and undergraduates would generally lie entirely the
other way.'

Nor, we would add, is it only among the academic
authorities and undergraduates that the temptation
'lies entirely the other way.' Throughout the
whole social body, amid all classes of the community,—alike amongst those that have just sufficient, and those that abound in wealth,—the
temptation to become heedless and indifferent
respecting the conditions of others, so long as we
ourselves are able to live prosperously, is one not
easily overcome. There are persons in England
who are so wealthy that the income of each one of
them far exceeds the total of the incomes of more
than a thousand labourers added together ;—and not
only is this the case, but it is also true that whereas
each of these labourers has to work from morn to
eve in order to become possessed of a sum equal to
the one-thousandth part of the rich man's income,

the latter receives the salary he has inherited without being compelled to render any service to the social body in return for it. It would seem, therefore, only right and proper, since fate has been so kind to these, that they should show a spirit of consideration to their less fortunate brethren : and, no doubt, to a very great extent they do so, but it is only by keeping alive in our midst the spirit of sympathy for those who have to suffer the hardships of poverty, that we can prevent the spectacle of a 'sublime indifference,' and the dangers that must inevitably result therefrom, for it is precisely this 'sublime indifference' which begets social warfare and revolution. There is a mystical Persian apologue which appears to us to be very significant and full of the allegorical wisdom of the East :—

'One knocked,'—it tells us,—'at the Beloved's door : and a voice asked from within, Who is there ? and he answered, It is I. Then the voice said, This house will not hold me and thee. And the door was not opened. Then went the Lover into the desert, and fasted and prayed in solitude. And after a year he returned and knocked again at the door. And again the voice asked, Who is there? And he said, It is Thyself! and the door was opened to him.'—

We may, indeed, refuse for a while to listen to the claims of the destitute and the poorer classes, but if a time arrives when a social war is threatened, and the unpleasant sounds of an approaching revolution grow daily and hourly more significant and distinct, then comes the knock at the door with the words, It is Thyself! Then a voice tells us that the interests of the poorest and most destitute classes are also our own interests, for no portion of the social body can, for long, be dangerously diseased without serious risk to the other members of the society of which it forms a part. Dean Church, it will have been noticed, implies (in the extract from his review given above) that there was in Clough's pamphlet *On Retrenchment at Oxford*, a tendency to socialism, but it must be remembered that at the time it was written the people in Ireland were dying on the roadside of starvation, and when food was placed at certain stations for them to fetch, many of them had already grown so weak that they were unable to crawl to the food, and died on the way. Clough's heart and feelings were stirred by so terrible a calamity, and he wrote this very earnest and eloquent appeal to the members of the University, praying that they would stint themselves as regards their pleasures and expenditure, and contribute their savings to the poor famished Irish men and women. 'In any case and every case,' he writes, 'let not the sky which in Ireland looks upon famishment and fever, see us here at Oxford in the midst of health and strength, over-eating, over-drinking, and over-enjoying. Let us not scoff at eternal justice with our champagne and our claret, our breakfasts and suppers, our club-dinners and desserts, wasteful even to the worst taste, luxurious even to unwhole-someness,—or yet again by our silly and fantastic frippery of dandyism, in the hazardous elaboration of which the hundred who fail are sneered at, and the one who succeeds is smiled at.'

At the commencement of this monograph we intimated that there was a similarity between the characters of Clough and Charles Kingsley ; and it is interesting to note that at the time this pamphlet was being written by Clough, his brother poet Kingsley was writing letters to the Chartists under the *nom de plume* of *Parson Lot*, and was attending public meetings in London in connection with those

I

social agitators. At one of these meetings he had even declared that he was himself a Chartist, but it must ever be remembered that while Kingsley told the Chartists that he deeply sympathized with their sense of the injustice of the law as it affected them, he never omitted to attack, with all the vehemence of which he was possessed, the methods which they adopted to strengthen their claim for a reform of Parliament. His action in this matter was no doubt prompted by the same 'sympathy with the sufferings and the claims of the poorer and humbler classes of the community,' which led Clough to write the pamphlet above referred to. It need hardly be stated that, also, as regards Tractarianism our two poets were entirely agreed, as may be seen by the following extract from one of Kingsley's letters written about this time, when the Oxford Tracts were already a thing of the past, and when John Henry Newman, their founder, had sent in his announcement to Bishop Wiseman of his conversion to the Roman Catholic faith. Kingsley writes :—' Men dally with truth, and with lies. They deal in innuendoes, impersonalities, conditionalities ; they have no indicative mood—no I, no thou, whereby alone have any great souls conquered. . . .

The Oxford party might take a lesson here ; much more so that numerous youth, who, now that the Tractarians are tired of playing at Popery, are keeping Dilettantism's altar alight by playing at Tractarianism—the shadow of a ghost—the sham of a sham. Our intellects are getting beyond milk and water ; they are becoming mere gas and bottled moonshine, from Limbus Patrum and the land Plausible !'

In connection with this similarity between the characters and writings of Clough and Kingsley, the two following paragraphs respecting their views on the same subject, ' Life,' are given as an illustration of the resemblance between the two poets. The first paragraph is from one of Clough's letters ; the second is an anecdote, respecting Kingsley, told by Mr. Hughes.

' Are you aware,' writes Clough in a letter from America, 'that Life is very like a railway? One gets into deep cuttings and long dark tunnels, where one sees nothing and hears twice as much noise as usual, and one can't read, and one shuts up the window, and waits, and then it all comes clear again. Only in life it sometimes feels as if one had to dig the tunnel as one goes along, all new for oneself.   Go straight on, however, and one's sure to come out into a new country, on the other side of the hills, sunny and bright.'

'Mr. Hughes tells a characteristic anecdote of starting one winter's night with his friend Charles Kingsley to walk down to Chelsea, and of their being caught in a dense fog, before they had reached Hyde Park Corner.   'Both of us,' Mr. Hughes adds, 'knew the way well, but we lost it half-a-dozen times, and Kingsley's spirit seemed to rise as the fog thickened.'   'Isn't this like life?' he said, after one of our blunders, 'a deep yellow fog all round, with a dim light here and there shining through.   You grope your way on from one lamp to another, and you go up wrong streets and back again.   But you get home at last—there's always light enough for that!'

It was about a year after Clough had taken his B.A. degree that there occurred what was to him a sad and sudden bereavement—we refer to the early death of Dr. Arnold.   How deeply the young poet must have felt the loss of one who was so dear to him we can well imagine.   We are told that he was 'completely stunned by the blow, incapable of realizing or speaking of what had happened, and unable to rest.' The calamity had been entirely unexpected, for disease of the heart had suddenly carried off its victim at the premature age of forty-seven, when in the very prime of life. The story of this great man's death is a very noble and a very touching picture, and we record it as related by one who tells us that his admiration of Arnold's character was even greater than his admiration of his talents :—

' Our readers,' he writes, ' must pass a day with Arnold. They will see of how homely and plain a thread, to all appearance, it was composed. Only, to make it more impressive, the day we will choose shall be his last. It differs in itself in no respect from other days, except as it is more of a holiday, since it happens to be also the concluding day of the half-year. On the morrow he was to shake his wings for Westmoreland. The morning is taken up with an examination in Ranke's *History of the Popes.* Then come the distribution of the prizes, the taking leave of the boys who are going, and all the mechanical details of finishing for the holidays ; his usual walk and bathe follow ; dinner next ; when he talked with great pleasure to several guests of his early geological studies under Buck-

land, and of a recent visit to Naseby with Thomas
Carlyle. An interval in the evening leaves room
for an earnest conversation with an old pupil on
some differences in their views of the Tractarian
theology ; after which, the day rounds off with an
annual supper to some of the sixth-form boys.
Arnold retired to bed, apparently in perfect health.
But before laying down his head upon the pillow,
from which he was never more to raise it, he put
his seal upon this busy and cheerful day by an
entry in his diary, which (reading it as we now
read it) seems of prophetic import. Yet, in truth,
these transitions had become so familiar to him,
that in passing from what was most secular to
what was most spiritual, he was hardly conscious
of the change. He kept the communication between this world and the next so freely open—
angels ascending and descending—that he blended
the influences of both—of things temporal and
things eternal, into one consistent whole :—
' *Saturday Evening, June* 11.—The day after to-
morrow is my birthday, if I am permitted to live to
see it—my forty-seventh birthday since my birth.
How large a portion of my life on earth is already
passed ! And then, what is to follow this life ? How

visibly my outward work seems contracting and
softening away into the gentler employments of
old age.   In one sense, how nearly can I now say,
' Vixi ; ' and I thank God that, as far as ambition
is concerned, it is, I trust, fully mortified.   I have
no desire other than to step back from my present
place in the world, and not to rise to a higher.
Still there are works which, with God's permission,
I would do before the night cometh ; especially
that great work, if I might be permitted to take
part in it.   But, above all, let me mind my own
personal work, to keep myself pure, and zealous,
and believing—labouring to do God's will, yet not
anxious that it should be done by me, rather than
by others, if God disapproves of my doing it.'

' What a midnight epitaph !   How ominous and
unconscious ! How tender and sublime !   He woke
next morning, between five and six, in pain.   It
was *angina pectoris*.   At eight o'clock he was dead !'

There have been writers (though, happily, very
few in number) who have ventured to intimate that
in their opinion the influence of Arnold upon many
of his pupils, and more especially upon Clough,
was by no means an influence entirely beneficial.
We are not disposed to here enter upon a discus-

sion on so large a subject, and, indeed, it is not one which is capable of being treated with any satisfactory result, so long as party spirit and sectarian animosity obtain possession of the field. Rather in parting (so far as these pages are concerned) with one, whose memory we cherish and respect, will we quote the following sonnet as expressing our own views and feelings more eloquently than we could, perhaps, ourselves express them :—

'TO REV. DR. ARNOLD.

'Sound teachers are there of religion pure,
  And unimpeached morality :—grave men,
  Who wield a cautious and deliberate pen,
  And preach and publish doctrine safe and sure :
And many such, I ween, can ill endure
  The eagle glance of thy far-piercing ken,
  But almost deem thee from some Stygian den
  Of monstrous error sprung, obscene, obscure.
Well ! they may rail till they have rail'd their fill ;
  Only let me, by such sweet poison fed,
  Drink from thy clear and ever-flowing rill,
Refreshment and support for heart and head ;
  Oft disagreeing, but extracting still
  More food from stones of thine, than such men's bread.'
                                        JOHN MOULTRIE.

The death of Arnold seems to have been the beginning of a time of sorrow and mourning in the

poet's history, for in the following winter he lost
his youngest brother George,—and in the succeeding summer his father, who had felt very deeply
the loss of his son, after some months' lingering
illness, also died.

Of the happier incidents of Clough's later Oxford
life may be mentioned various holiday rambles in
Wales, in Cumberland, and the English Lake
district, and more especially in the Highlands and
other parts of Scotland.　To those who have made
walking excursions amid the delightful scenery of
these portions of the country, it would seem a work
of supererogation were we to expatiate on the
ecstatic enjoyment of life that thrills through the
limbs of the wayfarer as he wanders onward,
repeating, perhaps, those lines of Wordsworth :—

  ' The cataracts blow their trumpets from the steep,—
  No more shall grief of mine the season wrong :
  I hear the echoes through the mountains throng,
  The winds come to me from the fields of sleep,
      And all the earth is gay.'

Life has, we think, few pleasures to offer more
delightful than the healthy enjoyment of such excursions on foot through wild, mountainous districts,
such as lie to the westward of our own island.　To

Clough, who was an excellent climber of mountains, and who could never walk too far in a country he liked, this enjoyment must have been intense. Professor Shairp has recorded some pleasant reminiscences of his walks with the poet in Wales and Cumberland, which the reader will find at page 23 (vol. i.) of 'The Poems and Prose Remains.' He there states that Clough's 'eye to country' was wonderful, and that he knew the whole lie of the different dales relatively to each other ; every turn, beck, and bend in them. Of his visit to the Highlands we shall have occasion to refer later on in our chapter on *The Bothie*, some of the incidents and characters of that poem having been suggested by actual scenes which he witnessed in the remote parts of Scotland.

And now, in bringing this sketch of Clough's Oxford life to a close, we would add a few words respecting his action in resigning his Fellowship at Oriel, which may be said to have terminated his University career. It should be remembered that in the autumn of 1845 he lost (so to speak) his friend Ward, who went over to the Church of Rome as soon as John Henry Newman had announced his intention of doing so. Clough, in a letter written about that time, states :—' A great many will be rendered uneasy by his (Newman's) departure, and one may look out for changes in one way or other,—it will be 'dropping weather' in the Romanizing line for some time to come, I dare say.' In the same year Mr. Matthew Arnold had joined Clough as one of the Fellows of Oriel, and in the year following, 1846, Clough had made the acquaintance of Mr. James Martineau, whom, he observed, he greatly liked, adding, that his forehead had a good deal of ' that rough-hewn mountainous strength which one used to look at when at lesson in the library at Rugby not without trembling.' In 1847 Ralph Waldo Emerson came over from America to deliver lectures in this country, and as his recently published biography by Mr. W. G. W. Cooke states, ' spent some time with Carlyle in his own house, and also visited Wordsworth and Miss Martineau at Rydal Mount.' Mr. Cooke adds that Emerson ' met Arthur Hugh Clough at Oxford and in Paris, and became much interested in that singularly original genius.' The intimacy between them was no doubt strengthened by Clough's acquaintance with America, and by the similarity in their views on many important subjects. In Paris they dined together daily during the month Emerson remained in that city.

The influence of men like Mr. M. Arnold, Mr. James Martineau, and Mr. Emerson, did not probably alter in the slightest degree Clough's opinions as regards the various dogmas of religion, but it did probably strengthen his own state of uncertainty respecting some of the fundamental tenets of Christianity, and brought the question of his own belief, or disbelief, continually to the front. The result, as we know, was, that he entertained doubts as to the fitness and honesty of his retaining his position as a tutor at Oxford, and that he eventually decided on sending in his resignation. He could not reconcile it with his conscience to continue holding a post which might be taken as implying religious beliefs which he was unable to avow. When, however, one remembers the number of Fellows and Tutors of Colleges who have held views far in advance of those held by Clough at this time, it seems necessary to inquire whether they have shown a want of honesty in not resigning, or Clough an excess of conscientiousness, and over-refinement, in determining to relinquish a post which, from a monetary point of view, he could ill afford to give up. But these are questions which each person must decide for himself, and, as in the case of the recent retirement of the Rev. Stopford Brooke from the Church of England, while some will hold that such retirement is an anachronism, and altogether unnecessary, others will agree with Clough and Mr. Stopford Brooke (whose views appear to be very similar to those held by the poet) that it is the duty of everyone to retire from a post, if to retain it would imply religious beliefs which he is unable to avow. For our own part, we think that it is equally wrong and dishonest for a Roman Catholic, a Dissenter, or a Deist, to remain in any employment, either as a tutor or priest, in which he is paid to teach and preach the very doctrines of the Church of England which he does not accept. But whether this would apply to an Oxford tutorship, such as Clough held, is a different question, for lectures on the poets and other writers of ancient Greece and Rome need not necessarily contain any reference to the *Thirty-nine Articles*, or the *Athanasian Creed*.

Dean Stanley, in writing about this period of Clough's life, stated that 'when at last he broke away from the University and the Church, it was with the delight of one who had known more than

other men the weight of the yoke which ecclesiastical authority had once laid upon him.' This
statement, however, brought down upon the late
Dean of Westminster a rather sharp reprimand
from another dignitary of the Church, the present
Dean of St. Paul's, who wrote,—' It is not, we trust,
inconsistent with sincere respect for the high
character borne by the writer of the above lines to
express a doubt, whether his own mind is incapable
of instituting that rigorous analysis, of which he
speaks, in any case which touches so nearly the
credit of his own personal friends. . . . . If we are
in any degree to avail ourselves of Clough's poetry ;
if his verse be in truth (as we cannot but believe)
the expression of his real thoughts and feelings,
then we must say that we have been unable in the
Bothie, in the *Ambarvalia*, or in the poems now
published since the author's death, to find one
single line that can be held to corroborate Dr.
Stanley's assertion that Clough 'broke away from
the University and the Church—with delight.' '

The following excerpt from a letter written by
Clough to Mr. T. Arnold is a striking commentary
on this Battle of the Deans, and would seem to
prove that Dean Stanley was right, after all. ' I

have given,' Clough writes, ' our Provost notice of my intention to leave his service (as Tutor) at Easter. *I feel greatly rejoiced to think that this is my last term of bondage in Egypt,* though I shall, I suppose, quit the fleshpots for a wilderness, with small hope of manna, quails, or water from the rock.' And again he writes : ' One may do worse than hire one-self out as a common labourer ; 'tis at any rate honester than being a teacher of XXXIX Articles!' And to Professor Shairp he writes : ' Another three weeks will see me at the end of these tutorial— what shall I call them ?—wearinesses, now at any rate. But whither the emancipated spirit will wing its flight can't be guessed.'

Moreover the *Bothie* (to which Dean Church refers) was written in September, 1848, a few months after Clough's resignation of his Tutorship, and it is the most mirthful of all his poems, and is, indeed, one long pæan, or song of liberty and delight, than which no better proof could be produced of the happiness he had won by doing what his (perhaps too sensitive) conscience had told him was his duty, namely, to retire from any apparent connection with a creed which, in his inmost heart, he knew to be no longer his.

As we have said, the *Bothie of Tober-na-Vuolich* was written and published immediately after his quitting Oxford, but before proceeding to speak of that poem we must glance briefly at the volume of lyric verse entitled *Ambarvalia*, as these poems were written during the time he resided at Oxford, although not published for some months after the *Bothie*.

Chapter IV.

AMBARVALIA.

THE volume entitled *Ambarvalia* was the joint production of Clough and his early friend and schoolfellow, Thomas Burbidge—now the Rev. Canon Burbidge, LL.D., Chaplain at Palermo,—the *Sicilian Shepherd* referred to in some of Clough's Oxford letters. It was published in 1849, and as Mr. F. T. Palgrave has observed in the Memoir prefixed to the poems published in 1862, it contains several pieces of which it has been justly said 'that they will hold their place beside those of Tennyson and Browning.' Respecting Canon Burbidge's contributions we are not called upon to offer any criticism or observations, and shall therefore confine our remarks entirely to those of his more illustrious fellow-labourer in the rich demesne of poesy.

In the earlier pages of this monograph a few examples were given of Clough's juvenile compositions which were written while he was still a school-

boy at Rugby ;—and on turning to the poems composed at the University, we find that the first fact
which appears especially noteworthy is that from the
time he left Rugby, and went into residence at Balliol,
in October, 1837, up to the year 1840, he may almost
be said to have written no poetry at all.   The first
three years of his Oxford life were poetically unpro-
ductive; but those who have themselves been undergraduates, and have experienced the busy time in
which chapels, lectures, luncheons, boating, wines,
&c., succeed each other in the noisy presence of
numberless companions, will not be surprised at
this.   In one of the poems in *Ambarvalia* the poet
gives us a graphic picture of his own history in this
respect.   He writes:—

> 'Roused by importunate knocks
> I rose, I turned the key, and let them in,
> First one, anon another, and at length
> In troops they came ; for how could I, who once
> Had let in one, nor looked him in the face,
> Show scruples e'er again ?   So in they came,
> A noisy band of revellers,—vain hopes,
> Wild fancies, fitful joys ; and there they sit
> In my heart's holy place, and through the night
> Carouse, to leave it when the cold grey dawn
> Gleams from the East, to tell me that the time
> For watching and for thought bestowed is gone.'

In these lines, as in nearly all Clough's compositions, there will be noticed a twofold meaning, an under-current of thought,—in his own words

> 'a vein of ore
> Emerging now and then on Earth's rude breast,
> But flowing full below.'

In this respect, and by their actuality and sincerity, they are distinguished in a marked manner from the productions of the multitude of poets who throng the lower ridges of Parnassus, but fail to reach the clear, bracing atmosphere of the topmost peaks. It has been said of the sonnets of Shakespeare that they are, as it were, 'double shotted with thought,' and it would seem to be true of the highest and best poetry of all nations that while the eye and ear are being charmed, respectively, by wondrous pictures of life, and by rare melody of language,—by the shapes and sounds of beauty,— the mind finds that it is being stored and enriched by the wisdom and thought of one who has pierced deeper than most men into the facts of the universe and the mysteries of life, and whose vision is bounded by a far wider horizon than that which is scanned by the large majority of mankind. It is not the lack of leisure for tuning, for tinkering, and polish-

ing his verse, that the poet laments, but (as in
the lines just quoted) the want of 'time for watching
and for thought.' Yet both of these are necessary
—both wisdom and a knowledge of the laws of
rhythm and metre, of the colouring and chiar-
oscuro of poetry ; and Clough appears to have been
thoroughly aware of this, nor was he by any means
a despiser of *style.*—' People,' he writes, ' talk
about style as if it were a mere accessory, the
unheeded but pleasing ornament, the mere put-on
dress of the substantial being, who without it is
much the same as with it. Yet is it not intelligible
that by a change of intonation, accent, or it may be
mere accompanying gesture, the same words may
be made to bear most different meanings ? What is
the difference between good and bad acting but
style ? and yet how different good acting is from
bad ! On the contrary, it may really be affirmed that
some of the highest truths are only expressible to us
by style, only appreciable as indicated by manner.'

Clough's most intimate friend, Mr. M. Arnold,
is, as we all know, a master of style,—and this is
not only true of his prose-writing, which is, perhaps, more striking than that of almost any other
author at the present time, but it is also equally

true as regards his poetry. The latter is gradually attaining that high position in the opinion of the critics which it so well deserves, and there are those who hold that the words which he recently wrote respecting the poet Keats, *He is with Shakespeare*, are, in a measure, applicable to himself. The style which characterizes Clough's compositions in verse is very dissimilar from that of his friend, and yet it is by no means improbable that hereafter these two Oxford poets will still be associated together as having given 'the truest expression in verse of the moral and intellectual tendencies, the doubt and struggle towards settled convictions of the period in which they lived.' Mr. R. H. Hutton has already, in his *Theological and Literary Essays* (page 256, vol. ii.), drawn a comparison between them, and his observations are in accordance with our own views. He states :—' Mr. Matthew Arnold and Clough both represent the stream of the modern Oxford intellectual tradition in their poems, but how different is their genius. With all his intellectual precision, there is something of the boyishness, of the simplicity, of the vascular Saxon breadth of Chaucer's poetry in Clough ; while Mr. Arnold's poetical ancestor is certainly no earlier than

Wordsworth. There are both flesh and spirit, as
well as emotion and speculation, in Clough ; while,
in Mr. Arnold, soul and sentiment guide the emotion and the speculation. There is tenderness in
both ; but Clough's is the tenderness of earthly
sympathy, and Mr. Arnold's the lyrical cry of
Virgilian compassion. Both fill half their poems
with the most subtle intellectual meditations ; but
Clough leaves the problems he touches all but
where they were, not half settled, reproaching himself for mooning over them so long ; while Mr.
Arnold finds some sort of a delicate solution, or
no-solution, for all of them, and sorts them with the
finest nicety. Finally, when they both reach their
highest poetical point, Mr. Arnold is found painting
lucidly in a region of pure and exquisite sentiment,
Clough singing a sort of pæan of buoyant and
exultant strength :—

> ' But, O, blithe breeze, and O, great seas,
>   Though ne'er, that earliest parting past,
> On your wide plain they join again,
>   Together lead them home at last !
>
> One port, methought, alike they sought,
>   One purpose hold where'er they fare.
> O, bounding breeze, O rushing seas,
>   At last, at last, unite them there ! '

These lines quoted by Mr. Hutton form the two concluding verses of Clough's fine poem, *Qua Cursum Ventus*, which has been the most generally and deservedly admired of all the pieces included in the *Ambarvalia*. It represents the accidental estrangement of two friends, who, after a brief absence, meet once more, only to find that their sympathies, views, and opinions have in that short separation been moving in opposite directions, and have become irremediably parted. The friends are depicted under the similitude of two ships lying side by side becalmed as the shades of night come on ; in the ' darkling hours ' the breeze, which had set in during the night, bears them far away from each other, and at dawn they are ' long leagues apart.' The whole of the poem, with, perhaps, the exception of the third verse, which is slightly unrhythmical, is excellent, and few persons, we imagine, have ever read it without feeling enriched and strengthened by the perusal, as though they had been breathing the pure, oxygenous mountain-breezes. The fifth verse, which we will quote in parting with this noble poem, is one to be remembered,—nay, rather it is one that, once read, can never be forgotten :—

'To veer, how vain ! On, onward strain,
    Brave barks ! In light, in darkness too,
Through winds and tides one compass guides—
    To that, and your own selves, be true.'

Of the other poems in *Ambarvalia* (and we can,
of course, only refer to the most remarkable) *Qui
Laborat, Orat* is one that has been often quoted,
and with which most readers are probably well
acquainted. Professor Masson, referring to this
poem in a paper written some twenty years ago,
observes :—' Surely, it is a prayer, the general
solemnity of which so overtones the discords from
common belief which the expert ear may nevertheless detect in it, that *if read in the diary of an old
saint, it would seem not out of keeping.*' [The italics
are ours.] . . . . And he adds :—' As even in those
pieces where the sentiment is mocking or satirical,
one can discern the writer's natural theistic faith
inspiring the expression and giving it pungency, so
the poems which are truly most characteristic of
Clough are those in which this positive, or really
religious, faith allows itself more strongly and
directly, and the strange truth is hinted, that it is
jealousy for the purity of this faith, and nothing
else, that is the actuating principle in what others
would call his scepticism.'

But what is it, we would inquire, that constitutes the charm of this poem ? What is it that has won for this poem a holy niche and home in the hearts of all who have learned to cherish it as something sacred, pure, and good ? Is it melody of language, or shapes and sounds of beauty ? We think not, but rather thought and tone, united and harmonized by the sincerity and earnestness of the true poet as distinguished from the mere 'artist,' who (to use Mr. Gosse's words respecting Barry Cornwall) has 'nothing bardic or prophetic in his nature, is burdened with no special message to mankind, and gives no sign of ever feeling very strongly on any particular point or occasion.' But what is the 'thought' of the poem, and what is the 'tone' in which it is expressed ? We will quote three stanzas for the benefit of those who have not yet become possessed of Clough's works, and cannot therefore refer to the poem itself ;—they are the first, third, and fifth verses.

'O only Source of all our light and life,
   Whom as our truth, our strength, we see and feel,
But whom the hours of mortal moral strife
   Alone aright reveal !

      *   *   *   *

With eye down-dropt ; if then this earthly mind
   Speechless remain, or speechless e'en depart ;
Nor seek to see—for what of earthly kind
   Can see Thee as Thou art ?—

    *   *   *   *

O not unowned, Thou shalt unnamed forgive,—
   In worldly walks the prayerless heart prepare ;
And if in work its life it seem to live,
   Shalt make that work be prayer.'

The following account of the circumstances which
led to the composition of these lines has been
furnished by Mr. T. Arnold, and is not without
interest. He states :—'The writer well recollects
the occasion from which the latter poem—*Qui
Laborat, Orat*—sprang. Clough was staying a
night in his London lodgings. In the evening
before bed-time the conversation had turned on the
subject of prayer ; and it had been argued that
man's life, indeed, ought to be a perpetual prayer
breathed upward to the Divinity, but that in view
of the dangers of unreality and self-delusion with
which *vocal* prayers were beset, it was questionable
how far their use was of advantage to the soul.
Clough slept ill, and in the morning, before departing, gave to his host a sheet of paper containing
the noble lines above mentioned. In this original

copy there was some difference from the form which the poem wears in the *Ambarvalia*, and in the present edition. Besides minor variations, the second line in the sixth stanza, which now runs :—

  "Unsummon'd powers the blinding film shall part,'—

stood thus—

  "Raptures unforced shall trance the silent heart."

In this, as in so many of Clough's compositions, there is present a twofold quality—a dissatisfaction on the one hand, with the usual standard of our anthropomorphic religion, and a desire, on the other, to raise and ennoble it,—to both simplify and purify it. It was, if we remember rightly, the late Mr. Emerson who pointed out that the religion cannot rise above the state of the votary—that the god of a cannibal will be a cannibal, of the crusaders a crusader, and of the merchants a merchant—and this is no mere rhetorical phrase, it is a fact confirmed by the history of all nations. The first chapter of the Pentateuch relates that the infinite and eternal Creator of the universe made Man in His own image ; and the traditions and records of all countries,—especially of ancient Greece and Rome,—show that the people of past ages have almost invariably reversed this sentence, and have made their Gods in the image of a Man, after the fashion of their own intellects, and their own hearts, having the weaknesses and the imperfections of human nature strangely mingled with the holier attributes of the Deity.

It is to this anthropomorphic tendency of mankind that we owe the very diverse views dominant among different classes of society in England at the present time. Among the lower, uneducated, and uncivilized orders the belief still exists that there is a certain illustrious personage[1] having cloven feet, uncomfortable features, and a sable complexion, —whom, however, the natives of the Guinea coast usually represent as being of a white colour ;—while among the educated classes this degrading superstition is almost, if not altogether, a thing of the past. But old beliefs, we know, always 'die hard,' for of all learning the most difficult department is to *unlearn,* and it has been wisely said that the older we get, the more tenaciously we cling to our errors, as those weeds are most difficult to eradicate that

[1] 'The Aryan nations,' writes Professor Max Müller, 'had no Devil.'—And perhaps the possession of one is a doubtful advantage.

have had the longest time to root themselves :—nor do we thank the operator who comes to offer his services in removing the decayed opinions that have in past years been so serviceable to us in masticating our otherwise indigestible food. Yet from time to time these unpleasant spiritual operators *do* appear, and, however objectionable their visits may be, they serve as the purifiers and saviours of our social and moral organization. In all ages heroic souls, in advance of their times, are born and announce new and definite truths:—they are the men whose higher imagination and perception enable them to pass, to some extent, from the finite to the infinite, from the gross and earthly to the spiritual and ideal. As instances of such men may be mentioned Confucius, Socrates, Marcus Aurelius, Luther, Spinoza, Goethe as well as John Wesley, St. Evremond no less than St. Augustine.

Amongst these lights and leaders of the world there are various grades and degrees of excellence, and although we may not rank the poet of whom we write with the illustrious names to which we have just referred, there is nevertheless a kinship between him and them. He was dissatisfied (as they were) with the images and idols which he was called upon to worship, and he found a nobler and truer religion in his own heart than that taught and professed by those around him. In one of the *Ambarvalia* poems he writes :—

> ' I have seen higher, holier things than these,
>   And therefore must to these refuse my heart,
> Yet am I panting for a little ease,
>   I'll take, and so depart.'

   *   *   *   *

But no one, we think, has more accurately depicted the position which Clough held in respect of the religion and creed of the times in which he lived, than Mr. J. A. Symonds, in the following paragraph, which we quote from a paper published in the *Fortnightly Review :*—' Clough simply tried,' he observes, ' to reduce belief to its original and spiritual purity —to lead men back to the God that is within them, witnessed by their consciences and by the history of the human race. The primal religious instincts of mankind are apt in the course of centuries to gather round them metaphysical husks, which are partly protective of the germs within, and partly restrictive of their true vitality. Times arrive at which these outward shells are felt to have become too hard and narrow. They must then be broken through

in order to free the kernels that lie within them.
The most clear-sighted men at such periods try to
discriminate between what is essential and what is
unimportant in religion ; but the majority cling
always to the human and material rubbish with
which it is clogged, as if it were the very living and
life-giving divine truth. We might use Plato's
simile, and compare the present condition of the
Christian faith, as contrasted with the teaching of
its great Founder, to the Glaucus of the deep, who
rises overgrown with weeds and shells from the
ocean, where he has been hidden. To pull away
those weeds, and to restore the god-like form to its
own likeness, is the desire of all thoughtful men
whose minds have been directed to religious questions, and who have not bound themselves to support the existing order of things, or undertaken for
their own interests to solidify the prejudices of the
mass. Christ Himself, by his answers to the questions of the Jews, taught us the principle of returning to simplicity in religious beliefs. He also, by
His example, justified us in assuming that the
Gospel is not stationary, but progressive ; that we
may come to know more of God than we knew
centuries ago ; and that the human race, by

extending its intelligence, extends its spiritual insight.'

It is a good thing that we have in Clough at least one poet—and it is, perhaps, not easy to find another—who has persistently in his compositions directed the attention of his readers to the really vital religious questions of our day. There are many amongst us who feel the same difficulties that he felt, are moved by the same desire to have the truth alone for the foundation of our faith, and are almost despairing that we shall ever live to see the tares of error that have been sown in the dark ages of Christianity uprooted and separated from the pure wheat of Christ's own teaching ;—it is well, therefore, that we should have one poet to whose writings we can turn for sympathy and instruction, for solace and light, in the hours of darkness and the passing moments of despondency. And where, we would ask, shall we find, at such times, a better anodyne for our pain, or a sweeter re-assurance of the ultimate victory of true religion over idle superstition, than in Clough's well-known poem, *The New Sinai*, which, in the *Ambarvalia*, bore the less suitable title of *When Israel came out of Egypt?* The first verse, as many will remember, begins with these soul-animating lines, this trumpet-call to the weaker-hearted, and to those who are still placidly slumbering in their tents :—

> ' Lo, here is God, and there is God !
>   Believe it not, O Man ;
> In such vain sort to this and that
>   The ancient heathen ran :
> Though old Religion shake her head,
>   And say in bitter grief,
> The day behold, at first foretold,
>   Of atheist unbelief :
> Take better part, with manly heart,
>   Thine adult spirit can ;
> Receive it not, believe it not,
>   Believe it not, O Man !'

In the succeeding stanzas of the poem Clough traces the religious history of the world, and the various forms of belief which have followed the progress and spiritual enlightenment of the ages as they have advanced and become wiser and more civilized. At first, in their darkness, he tells us, they were ready to accept whomsoever the prophet-tongues proclaimed, and eager to cry,

> ' 'Tis he,—the king is here :'—

But still,

> ' The long procession moveth on,
>   Each nobler form they see,

> With changeful suit they still salute,
>   And cry, ''Tis he, 'tis he !''

From the Gods of Olympus, and the polytheism ot
Greece, with the sacrifices of a thousand altars, he
passes to the smoke rising from Sinai's top,—to
the lightning and thunder amidst which

> 'a trumpet spoke,
>   And God said, 'I am One.''

Then from the past the poet proceeds to the latest
doctrines of his own times, to the dogmatic denial
of the existence of the Deity ;—and of these he
observes that they are but the clouds that wrapt the
Mount around : and he asks, is there no prophet-
soul who will dare, sublimely meek, to seek the
Deity within this shroud of darkness ?—

> 'That soul has heard perchance His word,
>   And on the dusky air
> His skirts, as passed He by, to see
>   Hath strained on their behalf
> Who on the plain, with dance amain,
>   Adore the Golden Calf.'

While in the final impressive stanzas he not only
attacks those who proclaim that there is neither God
nor Truth, but he attacks also the 'prophet's
brother-priest' who, deluding and deluded, urges

the people to adore the Gods, 'that safety give,'—
to fall down 'before the gilded beast.' The poem
closes with the following lines :—

> ' Devout, indeed ! that priestly creed,
>   O Man, reject as sin ;
> The clouded hill attend thou still,
>   And him that went within.
> He yet shall bring some worthy thing
>   For waiting souls to see :
> Some sacred word that he hath heard
>   Their light and life shall be ;
> Some lofty part, than which the heart
>   Adopt no nobler can,
> Thou shalt receive, thou shalt believe,
>   And thou shalt do, O Man !'

It were hardly too much to say of this poem that,
as indicating a new high-water mark of religious
thought in England, it is one of the most remarkable compositions of this century. One has but to
compare it with Byron's *Prayer of Nature*, written
a few years before Clough was born, to see what
an advance along the road that leads to true
nobility, to the higher spirituality, and worthier con-
ceptions of the Divine life, had been made in the
period that intervenes between the dates of the two
poems. As some may not have Byron's works at

hand, we will give the first stanza of his poem to show more plainly what the difference is to which we refer :—

> ' Father of Light ! great God of Heaven !
>   Hear'st thou the accents of despair ?
>   Can guilt like man's be e'er forgiven ?
>   Can vice atone for crimes by prayer ? '

It is apparent to all, and at once, that it were almost impossible for the later poet to have written these verses, or anything at all like them ; and, indeed, one might imagine that they were the productions of different centuries, whereas Clough was already in his sixth year, when Lord Byron died at Missolonghi ; and the former was only twenty-five years of age when this poem, *The New Sinai*, was written.

There are several other compositions included in the *Ambarvalia* that are deserving of notice, as, for instance, *The Questioning Spirit*, which, as the reviewer of the *Athenæum* complained, was wanting in clearness, but is now perfectly plain and intelligible to readers who have Clough's other works before them. ' It is,' writes Professor Sellar respecting this poem in the *North British Review* for November, 1862, 'it is one of the most beautiful of the early poems, both in thought and expression ; but it is one of the very few that appear to us to recall something of a Tennysonian echo.' This is true, for there are one or two lines in *The Questioning Spirit* which clearly remind the reader of similar sounds and phrases in *The Lotos Eaters*, but taken as a whole it is as distinctly marked by the individuality and original genius of the author as is Shelley's *Sensitive Plant,* or Keats' *Ode To a Nightingale.* And we would take this opportunity of stating that there are few poets who are less indebted to the writings of their contemporaries, or of the bards of old, than is the poet of whom we write. It is, however, a truism that every author is to some extent a borrower : and even Milton is no exception, but rather a striking example of this rule. Wordsworth, too, has much to be thankful for as regards the felicities of phrase and melody which he had learnt from studying the works of Burns and Cowley. But all poets of a high order put their own mark, the signet of their own individuality, on their compositions, and this Clough has done not only on the poems referred to above, but on nearly all his writings.

In concluding this chapter on the *Ambarvalia*

it remains to call the reader's attention to the lines *Come back again, my olden heart*, to *Sic Itur*, and especially to the spirit of sceptical sarcasm in the poem entitled *Duty*, one of the most remarkable of all the poet's compositions. It must not, however, be thought that Clough always wrote on philosophical questions; he was, in truth, a philosopher, but he was ' a man for a' that,' and we will bring our remarks to a close with the first stanza of a poem in which the man and not the philosopher has got possession of the pen :—

'Ο Θεὸς μετὰ σοῦ !¹

' Farewell, my Highland lassie ! when the year returns
   around,
Be it Greece, or be it Norway, where my vagrant feet are
   found,
I shall call to mind the place, I shall call to mind the day,
The day that's gone for ever, and the glen that's far away ;
I shall mind me, be it Rhine or Rhone, Italian land or France,
Of the laughings and the whispers, of the pipings and the
   dance ;
I shall see thy soft brown eyes dilate to wakening woman
   thought,
And whiter still the white cheek grow to which the blush was
   brought ;

   ¹ Ho Thëos meta sou—God be with you !

And oh, with mine commixing I thy breath of life shall feel,
And clasp thy shyly passive hands in joyous Highland reel ;
I shall hear, and see, and feel, and in sequence sadly true,
Shall repeat the bitter-sweet of the lingering last adieu ;
I shall seem as now to leave thee, with the kiss upon the brow,
And the fervent benediction of—' Ο Θεὸς μετά σοῦ !'

    *   *   *   *   *

Chapter V.

THE BOTHIE OF TOBER-NA-VUOLICH.

A LONG-VACATION PASTORAL.

'AND when I tell ye I saw a glazier,' writes Thomas Hood's Irish footman from Mont Blanc, 'ye'll be thinking I mane a fine boy walking about wid putty and glass at his back, and ye'll be mightily mistaken; that's just what a glazier (glacier) isn't like at all. And so I've described it to yees.' 'Even so say we of Mr. Clough's *Bothie*. When our readers hear of an Oxford poem, written, too, by a College Fellow and Tutor, they will naturally expect, as usual, some pale and sickly bantling of the *Lyra Apostolica* school; all Mr. Keble's defects caricatured, without any of his excellencies —another deluge of milk-and-water from that perennial fount of bad verses, which, if quantity would but make up for quality, would be by this time world-famous—and that is just what *The Bothie* is not like, 'at all at all.' '

Thus writes the late Charles Kingsley in a review of the *Bothie of Toper-na-Fuosich* [1] (The 'Hut of the Bearded Well '), which he contributed to *Fraser's Magazine* more than thirty years ago. The poem has been described as the author's 'Farewell to Oxford,' and Mr. Hughes states that 'he (Clough) would often tell in after life, with much enjoyment, how the dons of the University who, hearing that he had something in the press, and knowing that his theological views were not wholly sound, were looking for a publication on the Thirty-Nine Articles, were astounded by the appearance of this fresh and frolicsome poem.' The two epithets, which Mr. Hughes here makes use of—'fresh and frolicsome'— are, as the reader will presently discover, especially applicable to the *Bothie*. In it 'the joy of eventful living,' when the springtime of life is putting forth the buds and blossoms of youth, is so gaily depicted and with so accurate and masterly a touch, that one can with difficulty refrain from suspecting that the

[1] The word *Fuosich* would appear to be a mis-spelling for *Fiasaig ;* and *Toper* for *Tobar*. The name was afterwards changed to *Tober-na-Vuolich*.

whole poem—the entire story—is true from beginning to end, and that all the incidents, even
those of the smallest and most trifling description,
actually took place. The probability, however, is
that although many of the scenes were doubtless
witnessed by the author, and a few of the incidents
possibly formed part either of his own, or some
friend's history, the body of the narrative was invented by the poet and is pure fiction. Still, as
stated above, the account is so life-like, so realistic,
and so accurate, that few persons will read it without suspecting that there is far more truth in it than
is generally supposed. It was written at Liverpool
in the autumn of 1845, after Clough had left Oxford, and while he was still living at home with his
mother and sister, to whom he had been reading
Longfellow's *Evangeline*. That poem, and a re-
perusal of the *Iliad*, suggested the metre—namely,
hexameters—in which the *Bothie* is written. It
consists of about two thousand lines, and would appear to have been composed with almost marvellous
rapidity, for Clough in a letter to Emerson states
that it was only begun in September, and it was
certainly finished before the end of that month, as
it was printed, bound, and published by the end of

October. This accounts, in a measure, for the rough and rugged nature of some of the lines, but this ruggedness and wild irregularity of metre is in unison, in harmony, with the weird Highland scenery of the poem, and if the verse had been smoothed and polished, the effect would have been tamed down, and would hardly have been in keeping with that wild country—

' Where the great peaks look abroad over Skye to the westermost Islands.'

Before proceeding to the subject of the poem, we should mention that in the preceding summer Clough had actually been with an Oxford reading-party, like that referred to in the *Bothie*, to Drumnadrochet, in Glen Urquhart, and was thus well acquainted with the scenes which he depicted. It is said that he took the original name of the poem from a place by the side of Loch Ericht, a small heather-thatched hut, occupied by one of the foresters of the Ben Aulder forest. Possibly the ' Beard' of the Well was a growth of grass, or heather, adorning the space under the brink, or border, of the well. In any case the bothie, or hut, of the poem was the dwelling of one David Mackaye, blacksmith, and was situated amid the braes of Lochaber :—

> ' There on the blank hill-side, looking down through the loch
>   to the ocean,
> There with a runnel beside, and pine-trees twain before it,
> There with the road underneath, and in sight of coaches and
>   steamers,
> Dwelling of David Mackaye and his daughters Elspie and
>   Bella,
> Sends up a column of smoke the Bothie of Tober-na-Vuolich.'

After reading these lines one has no difficulty in depicting the bothie, raised a little above the road, with the hill behind it, the stream close by, the two pine-trees in front, and the ocean dimly seen in the distance. Perhaps one may forget its proper and poetic title,—the *Bothie of Tober-na-Vuolich*,—but, in that case, one can so easily substitute its other, and more prosaic, appellation of the *Bothie of What-did-he-call it !*

The preface to the original edition of the poem consisted of the following short paragraph, and is of importance as showing that Clough was fully cognizant of the metrical defects of the verse :—
' The reader is warned to expect every kind of irregularity in these modern hexameters ; spondaic lines, so called, are almost the rule ; and a word will often require to be transposed by the voice from

the end of one line to the beginning of the next.'
Such was the brief preface to the poem as it originally appeared in 1848, but it must not be forgotten
that many of the lines were afterwards altered, and
that many of the slight verbal defects of the first
edition no longer exist. The extracts given in
these pages are all taken from the last edition of
the poem as it appears in its improved and perfected form in vol. ii. of 'The Poems and Prose
Remains.'

The story of the *Bothie* may be briefly described
as being an account of an Oxford reading-party, one
of the members of which, Philip Hewson, the hero
of the poem, after two passing flirtations, finally
falls in love with Elspie, the daughter of David
Mackaye. The reading-party consists of the Tutor,
Adam,—and six pupils,—(six undergraduates,—
young, eager, exultant, from Oxford), whose names,
as given in the poem, are respectively Hope,
Lindsay, Philip Hewson, Hobbes, Arthur Audley,
and Airlie. The first stanza opens with the following lines, referring to some Highland athletic sports
which they had been witnessing :—

' It was the afternoon ; and the sports were now at the ending.
Long had the stone been put, tree cast, and thrown the
      hammer ;

Up the perpendicular hill, Sir Hector so called it,
Eight stout gillies had run, with speed and agility wondrous ;
Run too the course on the level had been ; the leaping was
     over :
Last in the show of dress, a novelty recently added,
Noble ladies their prizes adjudged for costume that was
     perfect,
Turning the clansmen about, as they stood with upraised
     elbows ;
Bowing their eye-glassed brows, and fingering kilt and
     sporran.
It was four of the clock, and the sports were come to the
     ending,
Therefore the Oxford party went off to adorn for the dinner.'

To those of us who are accustomed to the unreal
and artificial character of most modern poems, these
lines seem little less than a revelation, so strangely
natural, so wondrously real, do they appear :—they
are clearly very different from the verses and
poetry that now-a-days fill the pages of so many
dainty volumes of hand-made paper, with rough
edges, and spotless backs of whitest purity. But
we remember that when Mr. T. Arnold states that
in his judgment this 'Long Vacation Pastoral' is
by far the most perfect and precious monument of
his genius which Clough has left behind him ;—he
adds, that, 'although it differs widely from the

familiar type of modern pastorals, in which puling Damons and doleful Strephons talk unreal nonsense in the midst of a poetical scenery equally unreal, it is yet not unfitly called a pastoral, in so far as, like the idyls of Theocritus, it paints real life and natural feelings upon a lovely background of lake, river, and mountain.' There are other special qualities belonging to the poem, to which reference must be made later on, but this is the one particular characteristic which separates it in an especial manner from other verse, namely, the entire absence of anything approaching to artificiality, or unrealness, or 'sham' adventitious ornamentation. In this, too, it differs from Goethe's poem of *Hermann and Dorothea*, which, although a simple story of modern life, is strangely connected by the poet with the mythology of ancient Greece, and is divided into nine cantos, apparently because there were nine of the Muses, each canto being dedicated to one of those illustrious daughters of Jupiter and Mnemosyne, and bearing her name as its title or heading. Thus the first canto bears the name of *Calliope*, who presided over eloquence and heroic poetry ; the second that of *Terpsichore ;* the third of *Thalia*, and so on. To some readers this

formality and artificial decoration may possibly
have its charms, but others will prefer the simple
beauty of the *Bothie*, and will agree with Charles
Kingsley, who, in a letter to Professor Conington
written at Ilfracombe in December, 1848, observes:—
' I am game to 'go in' fiercely against all Ma-
nicheans, Hermann-and-Dorothea-formalists, and
other unclean beasts, to prove that Clough knows
best what he wants to say, and how ; and that taking
the poem inductively, and not *à priori* (as the
world, the flesh, and the devil take works of art),
there is a true, honest harmony, and a genial life in
it, as of a man who, seeing things as they were, and
believing that God, and not '*taste*,' or the devil
settles things, was not ashamed to describe what he
saw, even to Hobbes's kilt, and the 'hizzie's ' bare
legs.   All right ; manly, more godly, too, in my
eyes, than the whole moon-bewailing school of male
prude-pedants, who seem to fancy that God has left
this lower world since 1688, and would, if they
dared, arraign Nature as indecent, because children
are not born with shifts on.'   This last sentence, it
should be stated, refers to some foolish persons who
had charged the *Bothie* with indecency, chiefly
because of the lines respecting some young High-

land washerwomen whom one of the Oxford party
had seen at the town of Dundee, with

' Petticoats up to the knees, or even, it might be, above
   them,
Matching their lily-white legs with the clothes that they trod
   in the wash-tub !'

Surely, very harmless lines, as they seem to us
now-a-days, but thirty years ago readers were
possibly not so accustomed to references of this
kind, however purely and simply made, as they
have since become. But this is altogether a matter
of taste and custom which may be left to those
who are interested in such subjects.

Another important feature of the poem is the
vivid manner in which the characters are portrayed,
—each, and every one of them, standing forth as
clearly and plainly as though they were not only
living personages on the dusty high-road of life
with whom we had become acquainted, but were,
in addition to this, men and women of marked
character, distinct from the majority of mankind, who are often so similar that they appear
to have been made in one manufactory and
fashioned after the same model. Long before one
has reached the middle of the poem, each of the

M

Oxford party has become our intimate friend, whom we know almost better than we know ourselves, and whom we feel we should instantly recognize were we to meet him in the street. Even in the few lines at the beginning of the *Bothie*, briefly describing them as they descend from dressing, we feel that they are no longer strangers :—

—' Be it recorded in song who was first, who last, in dressing.
Hope was first, black-tied, white-waistcoated, simple, His
    Honour ;
For the postman made out he was heir to the earldom of Ilay,
(Being the younger son of the younger brother, the Colonel),
Treated him therefore with special respect ; doffed bonnet,
    and ever,
Called him His Honour : His Honour he therefore was at the
    cottage ;
Always His Honour, at least, sometimes the Viscount of Ilay.
—Hope was first, His Honour, and next to His Honour the
    Tutor,
Still more plain the Tutor, the grave man, nicknamed Adam,
White-tied, clerical, silent, with antique square-cut waistcoat.
Formal, unchanged, of black cloth, but with sense and feeling
    beneath it ;
Skilful in Ethics and Logic, in Pindar and Poets unrivalled ;
Shady in Latin, said Lindsay, but *topping* in Plays and
    Aldrich.
—Somewhat more splendid in dress, in a waistcoat work of a
    lady,
Lindsay succeeded ; the lively, the cheery, cigar-loving
    Lindsay,

Lindsay the ready of speech, the Piper, the Dialectician,
This was his title from Adam because of the words he
  invented,
Who in three weeks had created a dialect new for the party ;
This was his title from Adam, but mostly they called him the
  Piper.
Lindsay succeeded, the lively, the cheery, cigar-loving
  Lindsay.
—Hewson and Hobbes were down at the *matutine* bathing ;
  of course too
Arthur, the bather of bathers, *par excellence*, Audley by
  surname,
Arthur they called him for love and for euphony ; they had
  been bathing,
Where in the morning was custom, where over a ledge of
  granite
Into a granite basin the amber torrent descended,
Only a step from the cottage, the road and larches between
  them.
Hewson and Hobbes followed quick upon Adam ; on them
  followed Arthur.
—Airlie descended the last, effulgent as god of Olympus ;
Blue, perceptibly blue, was the coat that had white silk facings,
Waistcoat blue, coral-buttoned, the white tie finely adjusted,
Coral moreover the studs on a shirt as of crochet of women :
When the four-wheel for ten minutes already had stood at the
  gateway,
He, like a god, came leaving his ample Olympian chamber.'

These seem, all of them, living men, and their
individual characters become still plainer and more
fully developed as the story progresses, but they

never change : the Tutor is always 'the grave man, nicknamed Adam ;' Lindsay, always 'the Piper, the Dialectician ;' and Hewson, 'the Chartist, the poet, the eloquent speaker.' Moreover, there are various qualities, or virtues, scattered amongst them which were especially characteristic of Clough himself. Thus Arthur's love of bathing wins for him the title (which might well have been given to Arthur Clough) of the 'bather of bathers,' the 'glory of headers' :—Philip Hewson, the hero of the poem, is like its author, who was *certes* 'poet and eloquent speaker,' if he was not partly a Chartist also :—while Hobbes,

> ' contemplative, corpulent, witty,
> Author forgotten and silent of currentest phrases and fancies,
> Mute and exuberant by turns, a fountain at intervals playing,'

clearly bears some resemblance to Clough, who (as we are informed by Mr. Richard Garnett and others who had met the poet while living in London) was of a silent and retiring disposition, naturally somewhat shy and reserved, and yet at times exuberant, eloquent, discursive,—'a fountain at intervals playing.'

But to return to the subject-matter of the *Bothie*, —the first chapter, or canto, is mainly an account of the clansmen's gathering, and the dinner given in honour of the occasion, to which the Oxford party had been invited, and at which 'the grey but boy-hearted Sir Hector' presided, ' the Chief and the Chairman.' Here were gathered a strange assembly of pipers and targeted gillies, keepers, and peasants, —adorned with cairngorms and snuff-boxes,—a Catholic Priest and an Established Minister, the Factor, the Guardsman, Members of Parliament, the Marquis of Ayr, and Dalgarnish Earl and Croupier. After the dinner followed the whisky, the toddy, the toasts, the 'healths' drunk ' with all the honours,' and with these, most important of all, the speeches, 'the garrulous tale of Sir Hector,' and ' the gossip of neighbouring forests' told by the Marquis of Ayr—of which the poet observes,

' Bid me not, grammar defying, repeat from grammar-defiers Long constructions strange and plusquam-Thucydidean.'

Two of the orations, however, are given in full, but they are not very lengthy,—one being that of Sir Hector in which he proposes the healths of the 'Strangers,' the Oxford party ;—and the other being that of Hewson, ' the Chartist, the poet, the eloquent speaker,' in which he returned thanks for himself and for his companions, closing with covert satire, scarcely understood by his hearers, in the words :—

'I have, however, less claim than others perhaps to this
    honour,
For, let me say, I am neither game-keeper, nor game-
    preserver.'

So the dinner came to an end,—the feast was
over, and preparations were begun for the dancing
which was to follow. Thus the first canto concludes
with the parties retiring from the table, and as the
Oxonians are going out, we are told in words,
ominous and manifestly foreshadowing the future,
that as they quitted the doorway, a 'thin man, clad
as the Saxon,'—

' Singled out, and said with determined accent, to Hewson,
Touching his arm :—' Young man, if ye pass through the
    Braes o' Lochaber,
See by the loch-side ye come to the Bothie of Tober-na-
    Vuolich.' '

'Young man,' it is perhaps needless to state is a
favourite expression amongst the Highlanders ;—
and throughout the poem the Scotch character and
characteristics are carefully and skilfully delineated.
In some portions the scenes, are, indeed, painted not
only accurately, but also with almost Pre-Raphaelite
minuteness of detail. Thus in the description of
the clansmen's meeting, the poet is not satisfied
with the mere rough outlines of the picture,—the

superficial and general aspects of the assembly,—
but he must also paint-in the smaller and more
subtle characteristics giving local colour to his
poem, as in the line,—

' Pipers five or six, *among them the young one, the drunkard.*'

Mr. W. M. Rossetti has called attention to this in
a very excellent and able review of the *Bothie* which
appeared in the first number of that most interesting, though short-lived, periodical, the *Germ*, published in the year 1850.

In the second canto (like Goethe's *Hermann and
Dorothea*, the *Bothie* is composed of nine cantos),
the night, we find, and the dancing are over, but

' Morn, in yellow and white, came broadening out from the
mountains '

long ere Hope, Lindsay, and Airlie, had returned :—
Hewson and Arthur, with Adam, had on the other
hand got home by eleven, and had been bathing as
usual before breakfast. After the breakfast is over
the dialogue follows (which is the most witty
portion of the poem),—the famous conversation
on 'Woman,' clearly the proper subject for discussion on the morning after a 'dance.' The dialogue begins by Philip Hewson, the poet, the elo-

quent speaker, attacking ' fine-ladies,' and declaring
that did they know the grace, the attraction, that
labour adds to the beauty of woman, much waste
and loss would be saved us ;—and as he warms to
his subject, and grows fervent, impassioned, and
eloquent,—

' ' Take off your coat to it, Philip,' cried Lindsay, outside in
        the garden,
' Take off your coat to it, Philip.' '

But Philip was not to be silenced by persiflage
of this description, and nowise abashed proceeded
to extol the beauty of labour and real earnest
toil for the necessities of life, as compared with
the dreary inane existence of ' riding about in a
carriage,' and the 'utter removal from work, mother
earth, and the objects of living.'   As an illustration of the truth of his doctrine, he narrates how
he himself, once wandering through the village-
fields in the holidays, chanced to behold

                        ' a capless, bonnetless maiden,
Bending with three-pronged fork in a garden uprooting
        potatoes.
Was it the air? who can say? or herself, or the charm of the
        labour?
But a new thing was in me ; and longing delicious possessed
        me,

Longing to take her and lift her, and put her away from her
    slaving.
Was it embracing or aiding was most in my mind? hard
    question!
But a new thing was in me, I, too, was a youth among
    maidens.'

Thus he discourses, contrasting the reality and
natural beauty of the working poor with the artificial lives of the wealthier classes, adding,—'Better
a crust of black bread than a mountain of paper
confections.'

Here, however, the Tutor, 'the grave man, nicknamed Adam,' comes to the rescue of truth, to
fight on the side of 'fine-ladies;'—and urges the
impossibility of Equality, and the necessity of doing
our Duty in whatever station of life fate may have
placed us. He points to Nature as teaching the
vanity of the doctrine of equality;—for although the
daisy may not be so fine a flower as the carnation,
yet, he argues, if out of sympathy for the daisy the
carnation refused to expand to sun and genial summer, the poorer flower would lose thereby, and
would pray to the carnation,—

'Up, grow, bloom, and forget me; be beautiful even to
    proudness,
E'en for the sake of myself and other poor daisies like me.'

The time, however, had not arrived, the Tutor's logic notwithstanding, for Philip to be convinced ;—" Eat, drink,' he adds, ' eat, drink, and never mind others.'

Different, moreover, very different, is the view of Hobbes, who, starting up from the sofa, cries—

Philip who speaks like a book, (retiring and pausing he added),
Philip, here, who speaks—like a folio say'st thou, Piper?
Philip shall write us a book, a Treatise upon *The Laws of Architectural Beauty in Application to Women ;*
Illustrations, of course, and a Parker's Glossary pendent,
Where shall in specimen seen be the sculliony stumpy-columnar
(Which to a reverent taste is perhaps the most moving of any),
Rising to grace of true woman in English the Early and Later.
Charming us still in fulfilling the Richer and Loftier stages,
Lost, ere we end, in the Lady-Debased and the Lady-Flamboyant :
Whence why in satire and spite too merciless onward pursue her
Hither to hideous close, Modern-Florid, modern-fine-lady ?
No, I will leave it to you, my Philip, my Pugin of women.'

So the discussion progresses until at last it is brought to a close by Arthur, who reminds them that on the morrow they, or rather some of them, start on their travel for a three weeks' tour through the Highlands. Airlie, Hobbes, and the Tutor are to remain, however, reading at the cottage, and the latter warns Philip that ' he goes up for his examination at Easter, and must not therefore exceed the limits of his three-weeks' holiday.' The canto ends with the following observations from Hobbes, on the sofa,—Hobbes, so 'contemplative, corpulent, witty'—

—' Philip must hunt for that home of the probable poacher,
Hid in the braes of Lochaber, the Bothie of *What-did-he-call-it.*
Hopeless of you and of us, of gillies and marquises hopeless,
There shall he, smit by the charm of a lovely potato-uprooter,
Study the question of sex in the Bothie of *What-did-he-call-it.*'

The *Bothie* has been well described as an 'idyl of country life as fresh as a breeze of summer!' and in the third and succeeding cantos the truthfulness of this description is especially apparent, for in them are pictures of natural scenery, of rocky glens and foaming torrents, of 'lochs unexplored in the folds of great mountains,' of golden weather and heathery slopes, such as are, perhaps, not to be found in any other poem in the English language. And on this background are painted the romantic, homely, secluded scenes of the life and customs that meet the traveller as he wanders far away to the remote districts of the Highlands, where in the bright October,—

' Amid russet of heather and fern green trees are bonnie.'

Professor Sellar, writing in the *North British Review* some twenty years ago, observes with reference to this poem : ' No writer in prose or verse has shown so true a feeling of the beauty of Scotland, since Wordsworth gave a perfect voice to the music and pastoral loveliness of Yarrow. We feel, as we read, that a sympathetic mind is bringing us nearer than we ever were before to the grandeur and the force of Nature, as they are displayed in the rivers and woods of our inland Highlands, and over the immense range of the mountains, seas, and islands of the west.'

To return, however, to the subject, the story of the poem :—At the end of the three weeks' wandering, Lindsay and Arthur arrive once more at the cottage as arranged, but Hope had remained with an uncle for shooting;—'And Philip?' inquired the Tutor. Philip they had left in Rannoch, in a farmer's house by the lochside and the pines, helping to reap and 'bring in peat from the peat-stack.' Then follows an account of their travels which Lindsay gives to the Tutor,—'the Piper narrating and Arthur correcting.' This lengthy narrative brings them finally to the farmhouse, where Philip had been left, in Rannoch, and where they had all been detained by a storm. Here Philip had been smitten by the charms of the farmer's youngest daughter, a certain golden-haired Katie, and at a dance given by Grant of Glenurchie, had stayed dancing till daylight, and 'evermore with Katie.' And here they had left him lame, or professing to be so; and back to the cottage he came not, though Hope returned on the morrow, and to the Tutor's intense satisfaction informed them that Philip had gone from Rannoch.

But, at length, the absent hero writes and gives them the story of his adventures. He confesses to have been attracted by the maiden at the farm-house, yet, while walking alone in the neighbour-hood, a glance from a passing face appeared to warn and disenchant him, and he thereupon deter-mined to depart at once, and some three hours later he left, tearing himself away from the place. Afterwards, sitting alone in the mountains, he gives utterance to his sorrow in one of the most striking and pathetic passages of the fourth canto,—a truly noble lamentation, of which the following line, many times repeated, serves as the refrain :—

'Would I were dead, I keep saying, that so I could go and
    uphold her !"

In his letter to the Tutor he also expresses a fear lest his attentions may have done harm to the maiden, but he adds, ' No! she is purity ; I am the lost one.'

The reply of the Tutor is characteristic, beginning—

' Grace is given of God, but knowledge is bought in the market ;
Knowledge needful for all, yet cannot be had for the asking.'

It is, indeed, a homily in verse, imparting both wisdom and goodness to those who are prepared to abide by its teaching.

Shortly after this interchange of letters, to the surprise of all, Hope receives a missive from ' the Lady, his Aunt, at the Castle,' informing him that Philip had gone there to stay for shooting and dancing. The Tutor also has another letter from Philip, in which he confesses, *mirabile dictu*, that he is attracted by the beauty and grace of the Lady Maria, and recants all that he has previously said in favour of the poor and against the richer classes. It will be noticed that Clough has here displayed his most perfect and skilful irony, in making this young democratic Oxonian put forth such doctrines as that it is well that the mass, the

people, the majority, should remain bare and leaf-
less, suffering the pangs of want and poverty, if by
their so doing the social body can produce at its
summit flowers as 'lovely as the Lady Maria :'—
changed is now the burden of the enchanted re-
publican's song, while he sings,—

' Dig in thy deep dark prison, O miner ! and finding, be
    thankful ;
While thou art eating black bread in the poisonous air of
    thy cavern,
Far away glitters the gem on the peerless neck of a Princess.'

And to the rich—to the rich he sings so excellently,

—' Be rich, be sublime in great houses,
Purple and delicate linen endure ; be of Burgundy patient ;
Suffer that service be done you, permit of the page and the
    valet,

  *   *   *   *   *

Live, be lovely, forget them, be beautiful even to proudness,
Even for their poor sakes whose happiness is to behold you.'

Was ever irony more keen, or sarcasm more
piercing, or truth more sharply pointed to penetrate
the pachydermatous hide of a self-satisfied world !
And, moreover, it touches the most difficult of
social problems, respecting which the last word has
not yet been said,—the problem, namely, how the

injustice of fate or fortune, the indiscriminate dealing of good or ill luck with the accompanying birthright and inheritance of wealth or poverty, may best be met without injury to those various inducements to industry, without which the social machinery would soon cease to move. It is customary to draw a veil over these matters, and to avoid speaking too openly about what, however true it may be, is not the less unpleasant. 'Reconcile what you have to say with green peas, for green peas are certain!' Such, writes the late Mr. Bagehot, was Clough's idea :—'Taxes *is* true,' as the miser said. But if there is injustice in the world, staring society in the face, it cannot be got rid of by merely shutting our eyes, or holding our tongues. In the *Bothie* many of those social difficulties are referred to, some are discussed at length, and others form, as it were, the great 'under-song of sense' lying below the surface of the poem ;— but the reader must be referred to the work itself for further details.

In the last four cantos is given the history of Philip's final courtship and marriage with Elspie, the daughter of David Mackaye, of the *Bothie of Tober-na-Vuolich*. His flirtation with the Lady

Maria had not been of long duration,—he left the Castle in the course of a week, but the winged God of Love seems to have followed after his victim, and at last flower-crowned Hymenæus joined in the pursuit. Philip had not travelled far on his journey before one of the horses drawing the coach cast a shoe, and this accident brings him to the Bothie, where he recognizes his old acquaintance, the 'thin man, clad as the Saxon,' who had in the first canto invited Philip to pay him a visit :—also, in the daughter Elspie he meets once more the face that in passing had seemed to warn him to depart from the home of his first-love Katie. The story of their courtship, the doubts of Elspie, and the increasing love and passion of Philip, is told with much pathos, and many of the passages are both touching and truthful. The girl has especially the qualities peculiar to the Scotch,—she is canny and naturally prudent and provident ; even in the most impassioned moments of her wooing, the thought that seems to have obtained possession of her soul, looks towards the future, and ponders, and con- siders. In the following lines, for instance, her words in reply to Philip are such as only a Scotch maiden could have uttered :—

N

'And he continued more firmly, although with stronger
emotion :

Why should I say that I love, which I all but said to
another ?

Yet should I dare, should I say, O Elspie, you only I love ;
you,

First and sole in my life that has been and surely that shall
be ;

Could—O, could you believe it, O Elspie, believe it and spurn
not ?

Is it—possible,—possible, Elspie ?

Well,—she answered,

And she was silent some time, and blushed all over, and
answered

Quietly, after her fashion, still knitting,—Maybe, I think of it,

Though I don't know that I did : and she paused again ; but
it may be,

Yes,—I don't know, Mr. Philip,—but only it feels to me
strangely,

Like to the high new bridge, they used to build at, below
there,

Over the burn and glen on the road. You won't understand me,

But I keep saying in my mind—this long time slowly with
trouble

I have been building myself, up, up, and toilfully raising,

Just like as if the bridge were to build itself up without
masons,

Painfully getting myself upraised one stone on another,

All one side I mean ; and now I see on the other

Just such another fabric uprising, better and stronger,

Close to me, coming to join me : and then I sometimes
fancy,—

Sometimes I find myself dreaming at nights about arches
    and bridges,—
Sometimes I dream of a great invisible hand coming down, and
Dropping the great key-stone in the middle : there in my
    dreaming,
There I felt the great key-stone coming in, and through it
Feel the other part—all the other stones of the archway,
Joined into mine with a strange happy sense of completeness.
    But, dear me,
This is confusion and nonsense.   I mix all the things I can
    think of.
And you won't understand, Mr. Philip.'

This is a typical picture of a Scotch maiden,
and it is, as it were, made complete in the passage in
which Elspie compares Philip to the great strong
tide of the ocean, and herself to the little burn, or
rivulet, peacefully running through the glen :—

    ' I am but a poor slender burnie,
Used to the glens and the rocks, the rowan and birch of the
    woodies,
Quite unused to the great salt sea ; quite afraid and un-
    willing.'

But to proceed at once to the conclusion of the
story,—the courtship ends in a betrothal, and a
year later in marriage :—

' There in the bright October, the gorgeous bright October,
When the brackens are changed, and heather blooms are
    faded,

And amid russet of heather and fern green trees are bonnie,
Alders are green and oaks, the rowan scarlet and yellow,
Heavy the aspen, and heavy with jewels of gold the birch-tree,
There, when shearing had ended, and barley-stooks were
    garnered,
David gave Philip to wife his daughter, his darling Elspie;
Elspie the quiet, the brave, was wedded to Philip the poet.
So won Philip his bride. They are married and gone to
    New Zealand.'

It will be remembered that Clough stated that this poem was the result of his reading Longfellow's *Evangeline* aloud to his mother and sister; and Longfellow's poem was most probably suggested by Goethe's *Hermann and Dorothea.* If, however, we compare Goethe's poem to the *Bothie*, we are impressed by the wit, the vigour, the freshness, the rapid movement of the latter; while as regards the former we notice, in the place of these qualities, a calm, gentle, graceful domesticity, and we perceive the truth of Schlegel's criticism that it is a 'book full of golden precepts of wisdom and virtue.' It has been stated of Goethe that he was more Greek than German, but if we may judge by these two poems, the *Bothie* and *Hermann and Dorothea*, Clough was almost more Greek than Goethe appears to have been, for while the Oxford poem has much of the Homeric strength and vigour, the German is as placid as Goldsmith's *Deserted Village*, or his *Vicar of Wakefield*, to which latter work Goethe is said to have been introduced by Herder when he went to the University of Strasburg. 'Mr. Clough's hexameters,' writes Mr. Arnold in his *Last Words on Translating Homer*, 'are excessively, needlessly rough : still, owing to the native rapidity of this measure, and to the directness of style which so well allies itself with it, his composition produces a sense in the reader which Homer's composition also produces—the sense of having, within short limits of time, a large portion of human life presented to him, instead of a small portion.' And Professor Sellar, in an article in the *North British Review* for November, 1862, observes respecting Clough,—'No modern English poet is so truly Homeric,—not through conscious imitation so much as the gift of a kindred spirit,—in seizing immediately the real aspects and simple effects of Nature, which may be perceived and felt every day by the peasant as well as by the poet, but which are often lost from the excitement, the routine, and even the cultivation of modern life. Mr. Clough has much, too, of the spirit of that other ancient poet, who,

next to Homer, had the most vivid perception of
the outward world ; and who also has proclaimed,
with more power than any other, the majesty of
Nature's laws, and has penetrated more deeply
into that secret and all-pervading life :—

> "Cœli subter labentia signa
> Quæ mare navigerum, quæ terras frugiferentis
> Concelebras."

In one respect the *Bothie* is, indeed, *sui generis :*
for it is entitled to the honour of having been the
first successful poem *written in hexameters* in this
country.   The earliest use of hexameters by
modern European poets may paradoxically be
stated to be of very ancient date.   Some of the
very earliest (so far as we are aware) were written
in Hungary about the year 1540 by the poet John
Erdosi, who published a Magyar version of the
New Testament, prefixing a poem in hexameters to
each of the Gospels.   Klopstock is stated to have
introduced the use of this metre into Germany,—a
statement which is very easy to make, but very
difficult to verify without having *all* the earlier
German poems at hand to refer to.   Voss wrote his
Luise in hexameters, and that poem, as Goethe
acknowledged, suggested the composition of *Her-*

mann and Dorothea in the same metre. But although many poems have in Germany been written in hexameters, the number of those so written in England is exceedingly small. Sir Philip Sidney used the measure, but with little success; and Southey's attempt in his *Vision of Judgment* proved a decided failure. Coleridge's brief *Hymn to the Earth* beginning,

' Earth ! thou mother of numberless children, the nurse and
    the mother,—

contains some excellent lines,—one or two of them being almost suggestive of Mr. Swinburne's muse, as for instance,—

           —great mother and goddess,
Was it not well with thee then, when first thy lap was
    ungirdled,
Fair was thy blush, the fairest and first of the blushes of
    morning.'—

If one compares these with Southey's hexameters, we see at once what miserable failures the latter were, but then Southey states in the preface to his poem, that the word *Egypt* is the only spondee in the English language ! and yet some will think that *Egypt* is far more of a trochee than are such words as *husbands, sheepfolds, heartsease, harpoon,* and a thousand others. That the English language is unsuited to the measure is to some extent disproved by the fact that even in the Bible and Prayer-book many unconscious and unintentional hexameters have, as Coleridge pointed out, usurped the place of the ordinary decorum of prose, as in the two following examples :—

'Bind your kings in chains, and your nobles in fetters of iron.'

'Husbands love your wives, and be not bitter against them.'

Unfortunately the late Dean Alford did much to spread the opposite view that the metre will never be naturalized in this country. 'The objection,' he writes, 'against the hexameter is, in my opinion, a fatal one. It is not an English metre, and it never will be. All that has been done to naturalize it has entirely failed. The scholar can read it and enjoy it, but then it is on account of his knowledge of it in Greek and Latin. But the merely English reader can make nothing of it.' But in reply to this rash and ill-considered assertion the late Dr. Whewell observes—'All who have read English hexameters without prejudice, and noted their effect upon other readers and hearers, know that the facts are altogether at variance with Dr. Alford's statement. So far from all attempts to naturalize this measure having failed, it has been employed in several original poems which have very recently appeared, and which are very popular—'*Evangeline*,' '*The Bothie of Tober-na-Vuolich*,' and '*Miles Standish*,'—besides innumerable translations from the German,[1] and translations of part of Homer, which have had many admirers. So far from its being 'the scholar who can read and enjoy it,' and this on account of his knowledge of it in Greek and Latin, it is precisely the scholar who will not enjoy or tolerate it; and who, rejecting the best specimens of it, because they do not conform to Greek and Latin rules, demands a kind of hexameter in English which mere English ears will not tolerate. It is this demand 'of the scholar' for '*Virgilian*' hexameters which has, from the time of Sidney and Spenser to the present time, prevented this measure being accepted by the mere English reader, as it is accepted by the mere German reader since the time of Klopstock.'

The fact really is that few good English hexameter poems have, up to the present time, been

---

[1] Whewell had himself translated *Hermann and Dorothea* in hexameters.

written, but that they can be written is now manifest, for without referring to *Evangeline, Miles Standish,* or *The Bothie,* the two following passages may be quoted to indicate that English hexameters, when well written, are as beautiful as English iambics, anapæsts, or other rhythms. The first passage is taken from Clough's *Amours de Voyage,* and the second from Charles Kingsley's *Andromeda :—*

' Tibur is beautiful, too, and the orchard slopes, and the Anio
Falling, falling yet, to the ancient lyrical cadence ;
Tibur and Anio's tide ; and cool from Lucretilis ever,
With the Digentian stream, and with the Bandusian fountain,
Folded in Sabine recesses, the valley and villa of Horace :—
So not seeing I sang ; so seeing and listening say I,
Here as I sit by the stream, as I gaze at the cell of the Sibyl,
Here with Albunea's home and the grove of Tiburnus beside
    me ;
Tivoli beautiful is, and musical, O Teverone,
Dashing from mountain to plain, thy parted impetuous waters !
Tivoli's waters and rocks ; and fair unto Monte Gennaro
(Haunt even yet, I must think, as I wander and gaze, of the
    shadows,
Faded and pale, yet immortal, of Faunus, the Nymphs, and
    the Graces),
Fair in itself, and yet fairer with human completing creations,
Folded in Sabine recesses the valley and villa of Horace.'

*   *   *   *   *

(From Charles Kingsley's 'Andromeda.')

' Loosing his arms from her waist he flew upward awaiting the
 sea-beast.

Onward it came from the southward, as bulky and black as a
 galley,

Lazily coasting along, as the fish fled leaping before it ;

Lazily breasting the ripple, and watching by sandbar and
 headland,

Listening for laughter of maidens at bleaching, or song of the
 fisher,

Children at play on the pebbles, or cattle that pawed on the
 sandhills.

Rolling and dripping it came, where bedded in glistening
 purple

Cold on the cold sea-weeds lay the long white sides of the
 maiden,

Trembling, her face in her hands, and her tresses afloat on
 the water.

As when an osprey aloft, dark-eyebrowed, royally crested,

Flags on by creek and by cove, and in scorn of the anger of
 Nereus

Ranges, the king of the shore ; if he see on a glittering
 shallow,

Chasing the bass and the mullet, the fin of a wallowing
 dolphin,

Halting he wheels round slowly, in doubt at the weight of his
 quarry,

Whether to clutch it alive, or to fall on the wretch like a
 plummet,

Stunning with terrible talon the life of the brain in the hind
 head :

Then rushes up with a scream, and stooping the wrath of his
  eyebrows
Falls from the sky like a star, while the wind rattles hoarse in
  his pinions.
Over him closes the foam for a moment ; then from the sand-
  bed
Rolls up the great fish, dead, and his side gleams white in
  the sunshine.
Thus fell the boy on the beast ; thus rolled up the beast in
  his horror,
Once, as the dead eyes glared into his ; then his sides, death-
  sharpened,
Stiffened and stood, brown rock, in the wash of the wandering water.
  Beautiful, eager, triumphant, he leapt back again to his
  treasure ;
Leapt back again, full blest, toward arms spread wide to
  receive him.
Brimful of honour he clasped her, and brimful of love she
  caressed him.'

*   *   *   *   *

Both these passages are excellent, although the
latter would, perhaps, have been improved by the
use of a greater number of spondees, as in Clough's
line,

' Falling, falling yet, to the ancient lyrical cadence,'

which contains four spondees and only two dactyls.
Kingsley had, however, studied this question closely,

and had even made an analysis of six passages of
fifty lines each, taken respectively from Homer,
Lucretius, Virgil, Ovid's 'Metamorphoses,' Goethe's
'Hermann and Dorothea,' and his own 'Andromeda.' By this 'little bit of induction' (as he calls
it) he discovered that Virgil and Ovid used more
spondees than the rest, and that Homer in the
fifty lines had only forty-eight (not including the
terminal spondees). 'Therefore,' he adds, 'taking
Homer as the ideal, our English is not so far off, in
spite of its want of spondees. I took Goethe from
that exquisite opening of the third canto ; but I
must say that either I can't read German, or it
goes horribly like a cat in walnut shells quoad
rhythm. . . . . Virgil I took from that blasphemous
doggrel yclept the opening of the Georgics, and
between such bits as—

'Curs' atqu' aud', and
'Ingredere, et votis jam nunc assuesce vocari ;'

(the last four syllables of which only are not tor-
turing), and so forth. My teeth (I haven't many)
were pretty near broken by the time I had read
through the fifty lines. . . . . I must try for Homer's
average of a spondee a line.'

This proportion of a spondee a line will be found to be about the average number of spondees that occur in the *Bothie*, for Clough not unfrequently, in order to change the cadence of the hexameters, has placed a spondee in the fifth foot, as for instance in the line

' Sleeping in shieling and bothie, with drover on hillside
sleeping.'

This is a practice which all writers of English hexa-meters may possibly find very advantageous to adopt, as it relieves the ear when it is growing weary of the monotonous iteration of the hexametrical cadence.

Another practice which Clough uses with a very pleasing effect is the frequent repetition of the same line, or part of a line ; but in so doing he is only following the example of the Greek epic and pastoral poets. ' These repetitions act like the burden of a song, or the recurrence of the original air in music, after wandering variations. They make one feel, as in the old Greek poets, that the author is in earnest, and enjoys his conception, and likes to take it up, and play with it again and again, lingering over it almost reverently, as if

conscious that there was something more in it than
he could bring out in words.'

The American poet Edgar Poe has very successfully employed this practice in his poetry and has
added to it a method peculiar to his own verse,
which forms one of the most characteristic features
of his compositions. But the repetitions of Clough
have, too, a distinctive character of their own, the
nature of which can only be thoroughly understood
by reading his poems.

There has been great diversity of opinion expressed as to the rhythmic excellence, or the reverse, of Clough's hexameters : for while one writer
complains that they are rough, irregular, and un-
equal ;—another urges that they are unlike those
of any other writer in any language, and better
than those of any other English author ; and that
Clough takes a high place for the subtlety, variety,
and racy flavour of originality which he has imparted to this ancient vehicle of thought. These
two criticisms, taken together, contain the whole
truth of the matter, for some of the lines in the
Bothie are unquestionably difficult to scan, while
others are plainly metrically imperfect. Yet the
rhythm of the poem taken as a whole is wonderfully

effective ; nor, in reading it, do we remember to have met with such a terrible hexameter as that famous line in *Evangeline*,—

'Children's children sat on his knee, and heard his great
     watch tick.'—

It is, or it should be, a rule,—a *sine quâ non*,—of English hexameter verse, that it must, so to speak, 'read itself,'—and for the most part Clough's poem does comply with this requirement ; as also (though not always) with the rule that the first syllable of a line must never be weak or doubtful, never leave the reader uncertain whether it be a long syllable or not.   If the line begin with a tribrach, instead of a dactyl, its doom is sealed ; and if the cæsura be neglected, or trochees be used in the place of spondees, the effect will not be a happy one.   But they who wish to study the writing of English hexameters cannot do better than read the excellent translations of Homer by the late Dr. Hawtrey and Mr. Lockhart.   They will, perhaps, find it difficult to decide which of these two authors has been most successful in the composition of perfect hexameters.   Let these, too, remember that Clough has shown the *flexibility* of this metre, and that it is only stiff, wooden, and monotonous when badly written. An able writer has observed that 'it is perhaps the most flexible of English metres. Better than any others it changes from grave to gay without desecrating what should be solemn, or disenchanting that which should be graceful.'

But the last words on such a poem as *The Bothie of Tober-na-Vuolich* should not be respecting the minor merits of rhythm or metre, for these we can find in the skilful compositions of ordinary versifiers. Rather should they refer to the higher qualities, to the wit and humour and mirthfulness, as pure and fresh as the mountain breezes; to the simple 'truthfulness to Nature;' to the vivid flashes of genius lighting up large tracts of thought and philosophy, and illuminating the dark abysses of social, or metaphysical, problems; to the serious-ness, the earnestness, of a poet who had in his boyhood been the pupil and companion of Dr. Arnold; to the picturesque eloquence, to the rhetorical flow of words, to the creative and even fanciful works of the imagination, to the beauty, the sympathy, the delight, now pathetic, now simply poetic, yet always enchanting, of one who had listened, and not altogether in vain, to the preaching and graceful teaching of Cardinal

O

Newman.   But we have been told that, 'as in men, so in books, the soul is all with which our souls must deal; and the soul of the book is whatsoever beautiful, and true, and noble we can find in it.' The desire of the human heart is always for a higher ideal, a more beautiful life, a loftier aim or course of action, and some answer to such craving will be found in the poem of the *Bothie of Tober-na-Vuolich*, and in the passionate ardour of such lines as—

' O that the armies indeed were arrayed, O joy of the onset,
Sound, thou Trumpet of God, come forth, Great Cause, to
        array us,
King and Leader appear, thy soldiers sorrowing seek thee,
Would that the armies indeed were arrayed, O where is the
        battle?'

   *   *   *   *   *

Chapter VI.

LIFE IN LONDON.

LIFE in London! There is an inclusiveness in these words, a comprehensiveness so wide and varied, that although one can never see them written down without experiencing a sense of joy, our pleasure is, unfortunately, always accompanied by visions of pain and suffering. In London you may be living in the sunshine of peace and happiness, but is it not true that you must be careful not to enter into many of the streets,—and, indeed, into whole districts,—if you do not wish to have your own calm mood of 'sweet content' rudely shaken and disturbed? Thackeray loved London, and so do we ;—but could he walk, we would ask, direct from the British Museum to Whitehall without something like a shudder passing over him, not so much, perhaps, on account of the squalor, destitution, and misery which he would there behold, as on account

of the dressy pageant of sumptuous living to be
witnessed at no great distance from this very neighbourhood ? We walk in the Row during the season,
and we find it pleasant ; but would it be so, if our
minds were less influenced by the strange forgetful-
ness that can enjoy that scene within easy walking
distance of the districts referred to ? But 'fault-
finders should be fault-menders,' and we are by
no means prepared with a new, perfect, and practi-
cable remedy of our own manufacture, of this unsatisfactory and, as it is becoming, precarious condition of society. It is well, however, that we should
occasionally be reminded of it, and we must confess
our great unwillingness to rest satisfied with the views
put forward by Clough in the following extract from
a letter written by him during his residence in the
metropolis :—' It is a good deal forgotten,' he writes,
' that we came into this world to do, not kindness to
others, but our own duty, to live soberly, righteously,
and godly, not benevolently, philanthropically, and
tender-heartedly. To earn his own bread honestly,
—in the strictest sense of the word *honestly*,—to
do plain straightforward work or business well and
thoroughly, not with mere eye-service for the
market, is really quite a sufficient task for the

ordinary mortal.' This is as much of the letter as is given in 'The Poems and Prose Remains,' whence we quote it, and without seeing the context, the remainder of the epistle, one cannot judge what Clough really meant to imply by this philosophic sermonette so much at variance with his own teaching and practice. Doubtless he was aware, and it is scarcely possible that he could for the moment have forgotten, that he might have written with equal force, and far greater truth, that 'It is a *good deal forgotten!* that we came into this world to do, not kindness to ourselves, but to others,—not only our duty to ourselves, but also our duty to our neighbour,—to live not only soberly, righteously, and godly, but also benevolently, philanthropically, and tender-heartedly.' There is so much truth and intelligence in all Clough's observations, that one has no hesitation in deciding that there must have been some special circumstances, not recorded, which led him to thus expatiate on the sufficiency of doing our duty to ourselves ;—a doctrine very pleasant to contemplate, and one which the world is in little danger of forgetting.

It was in October, 1849, the year after he had relinquished his Fellowship at Oriel, that Clough

entered upon his duties as Principal of University
Hall, London, an institution founded for the purpose of receiving students attending the lectures at
University College. During the earlier portion of
the year he had availed himself of the leisure time
which intervened between his appointment to this
post and his taking office by making a visit to
Italy, and he was, as it so happened, present in
Rome during the time it was besieged by the
French. Mr. F. T. Palgrave, in a paper published
in *Fraser's Magazine* in 1862, writes: ' He (Clough)
was meanwhile spending the spring and summer in
Italy : drawn thither in part by the charm of that
country to so sympathetic a student of the ancient
literature ; in part by the attraction which any
effort to gain rational liberty exercises over all
noble natures. But he was destined to see barbarian
feet again planted on the Capitol. Unable or
unwilling to believe that what at least bore the
name Republic could really lead the crusade on
behalf of despotism, he lingered on till the invest-
ment of Rome by a French army rendered departure
impossible.' During the time he was thus im-
prisoned in Rome, he wrote his second long poem,
the *Amours de Voyage*, which will be referred to in

a subsequent chapter; and while at Naples, which he visited during the same tour, the striking religious poem entitled *Easter Day* was composed.

It should be here mentioned that in one of his letters written at Rome he refers to having made the acquaintance of Margaret Fuller Ossoli, the American poetess, whose genius was as rare as her fate was tragic;—the friend of Mazzini, of Emerson, and of Hawthorne, her dirge has been sung, how nobly! by Walter Savage Landor in those memorable lines which conclude with the words—

> ' Rest, glorious soul,
> Renowned for strength of genius, Margaret!
> Rest with the twain too dear! My words are few,
> And shortly none will hear my failing voice;
> But the same language with more full appeal
> Shall hail thee: the hour is come;
> Take we our seats, and let the dirge begin.'

In the autumn Clough returned to London, and went forthwith to reside at University Hall in Gordon Square. To him 'life in London,' after the enjoyment of foreign travel, and convivial days at Oxford, proved a rather dull and wearisome exist-ence,—' a loneliness relieved by evening parties,' he writes, ' is not delightful.' And Mr. Palgrave (in the 'Fraser' article referred to above) observes :—

'At first, indeed, he found in the Wardenship of University Hall, London, an employment not altogether congenial to his disposition; yet even here, in the comparative solitude of the new abode, the discovery that withdrawal from Oxford had no ways shaken the affection of those he trusted, and by degrees the prospect of what lay even nearer to his heart and happiness, cheered the hours which, to a disposition so tenderly sensitive as Clough's were apt to catch a gloom from the sight of unfamiliar walls and faces. In more than one set of deeply-felt stanzas in his *Ambarvalia*, he had expressed, at Oxford, the sinking of the soul at the severance which divergent opinion so often, within his own experience, had wrought amongst friends. But in the increased respect of those he most valued, whether alien from his tone of thought or not, he received now part of the reward with which truth recompenses self-sacrifice. Soon, too, when resident for a few months in America, whither in 1852 he went to try his fortunes in preparation for marriage with one worthy of him, he found amongst the most distinguished men of the Northern States a renewal of the deep interest which he had aroused in his earlier companions.'

Clough, however, does not appear to have been
long in making new acquaintances, and of these
should be especially mentioned that with Thomas
Carlyle, for whom he appears to have entertained
the warmest feeling of esteem and admiration.
'It is,' he writes in a letter about this date, 'rain,
rain, rain, and universal umbrellas travelling church-
ward.   I meant to get another walk to Chelsea to
see Mrs. Carlyle ; but the waters are covering the
face of the New Road, and the omnibuses, doubtless, would be full.'   Mr. Palgrave, too, occasionally
found his way to Gordon Square to breakfast with
Clough and his eleven undergraduates :—while in a
letter to Mr. T. Arnold we find a postscript stating,
'As in old times at breakfast in Oriel, so here for
an afternoon walk and dinner I am waiting for M.
and, I believe, E.'   [Mr. M. Arnold, we presume,
and his brother, the author of *The Light of Asia*,
and that sweet lyric, *À ma Future.*]   From these
epistolary references it would seem that the new
scene of life might have been far more solitary
than it really was ; and yet long days spent in
dreary teaching would be apt to become monotonous, and even in his most mirthful communications there is a tendency, during these years of his

life, to be slightly querulous and dissatisfied. He
does not, indeed, exclaim with Macbeth, ' I 'gin to
be a-weary of the sun !' but he does, forsooth, write
to Professor Shairp, ' We are still, I believe, travelling about the sun, round and round, round and
round, in the old foolish fashion. It is certainly a
very funny way for the *anima mundi* to amuse
itself. But *chacun à son goût!*'—Clearly life in
Gordon Square was not edifying, or very cheerful
in 1849, and, save for an Irvingite, it is not, perhaps,
the most heart-gladdening form of existence at the
present time. Clough remained a resident in the
Square during the three years he retained the post
of Principal at the Hall, and here were written a
few of his shorter poems, including *A London Idyll,
Say not the Struggle nought Availeth, Bethesda,
In a London Square*, &c. &c.

Of these, *A London Idyll* has a charm of its own
in that it is in a measure unique, for it is different
not only as regards metre, but also as regards
manner, from all of Clough's other poems. It was
composed in the spring of 1851, and a copy of it
was forwarded by the author to a friend in New
Zealand very shortly after its composition. If it be
compared with another, and earlier, ' Idyllic Sketch,'

the *Natura Naturans*, which was published in the
Ambarvalia, and ends with the lines

> ' Or ever yet to young Desire
> Was told the mystic name of Love,'—

it will be found to be distinguished by a strength
and character that we look for in vain in the earlier
composition. The following is the opening verse,—

> ' On grass, on gravel, in the sun,
> Or now beneath the shade,
> They went, in pleasant Kensington,
> A prentice and a maid.
> That Sunday morning's April glow,
> How should it not impart
> A stir about the veins that flow
> To feed the youthful heart.
>   Ah ! years may come, and years may bring
>   The truth that is not bliss,
>   But will they bring another thing
>   That can compare with this ? '

*　　*　　*　　*　　*

The refrain is very pleasing and musical ; it has
apparently suggested to Mr. Palgrave the following
charming refrain of one of his most successful
lyrics,—

> ' Then, 'mid the roses let us sing,
> As 'mid the roses they did ;
> For life will bring no second spring,
> When summer once is faded.'

The lines entitled *Bethesda* are connected, and should be read, with *The Questioning Spirit*, a poem which attracted considerable attention when first published in *Ambarvalia*. The philosophy of these two compositions is that of the school of modern Agnosticism, which has in recent years been accepted and taught by a large number of disciples, and has been ably defended by Mr. Leslie Stephen in a paper entitled *An Agnostic's Apology*, which he contributed to the *Fortnightly Review* in 1876. He writes :—' The word Agnosticism seems to imply a fairly accurate appreciation of a form of creed already common and daily spreading. The Agnostic is one who asserts—what no one denies —that there are limits to the sphere of human intelligence. He asserts, further, what many theologians have expressly maintained, that those limits are such as to exclude at least what Mr. Lewes has so happily called 'metempirical' knowledge. But he goes further, and asserts, in opposition to theologians, that theology lies within this forbidden sphere.' . . . And again—' The last English writer who professed to defend Christianity with weapons drawn from wide and genuine philosophical knowledge was Dean Mansel. The whole substance of

his argument was simply and solely the assertion
of the first principles of Agnosticism. Mr. Herbert
Spencer, the prophet of the Unknowable, the fore-
most representative of Agnosticism, professes in
his programme to be carrying 'a step further the
doctrine put into shape by Hamilton and Mansel.'
Nobody, I suspect, would now deny, nobody except
Dean Mansel himself ever denied very seriously,
that the 'further step' thus taken was the logical
step.' . . . . 'You tell us to be ashamed of professing ignorance. Where is the shame of ignorance
in matters still involved in endless and hopeless
controversy? Is it not rather a duty?'

Thus writes Mr. Leslie Stephen,—and it is,
perhaps, a thing not greatly to be wondered at, if
Agnosticism is, as he states, a 'creed already
common and daily spreading,' for the human race
has of late been discovering that in past ages it
has formed many hasty judgments, made many bold
statements, and many dogmatic assertions, which it
has had afterwards to greatly modify, or entirely
abandon as being simply untrue. Thus, for instance,
it has discovered that whereas as recently as some
thirty years ago it firmly believed, and as firmly
asserted, that the world was created just 4004 years

before the birth of Christ,[1] the science of geology has since proved that the world, and even the human race, have been created an infinitely longer period ; —while the teaching of Darwin, and the doctrine of Evolution now point to the possibility that the earth and her children may never have been created at all, but have been evolved, or, in other words, have grown, out of the systems preceding them. So, too, in respect of many other theories, we stand at last like a company of guessers who have failed to solve the conundrum, the riddle, which some subtle comrade has propounded to tax their wits ; one after another we have had our guess, and the retort, 'Wrong again !' has rung in our ears,—and now, at last we are content to give it up, and simply confess that we do not know.

And so, in the case of Clough, it is not surprising to find him writing in these two poems—

> 'But as the echoing chorus died away
> And to their dreams the rest returned apace,
> By the one spirit I saw him kneeling low,
> And in a silvery whisper heard him say :
> Truly thou know'st not, and thou need'st not know.'

[1] The precise date of the Creation as given in the Rev. Dr. John Trusler's *Chronology* (10th edition, page 72) was October 13th, 4004 B.C. !

And again—

> 'Were not things old once new ?—
> I know not, let me do as others do.
> And when the rest were over past,
> I know not, *I will do my duty, said the last.*'

Here we have the poet's answer to both Theologian and Agnostic,—to both dogma and doubt,—and that answer is,—

> 'I know not, I will do my duty.'

It is an answer which may be found written on the pages of many books, and few writers have given it more gracefully than Margaret Fuller Ossoli in the following paragraph and verses:— 'The stars tell all their secrets to the flowers, and if we only knew how to look around us, we should not need to look above. But man is a plant of slow growth, and great heat is required to bring out his leaves. He must be promised a boundless futurity to induce him to use aright the present hours. In youth, fixing his eyes on those distant worlds of light, he promises himself to attain them, and there find the answer to all his wishes. His eye grows keener as he gazes, a voice from the earth calls it downward, and he finds all at his feet :—

    ' Be to the best thou knowest ever true,
      Is all the Creed ;
    Then, be thy talisman of rosy hue,
      Or fenced with thorns that wearing thou must bleed,
    Or gentle pledge of love's prophetic view,
      The faithful steps it will securely lead.'

     *   *   *   *   *

But it must not be supposed as regards Clough that any unwillingness on his part to accept as final the theological or metaphysical creed, or doctrine, of this or that school of thought, prevented him from believing in the continuous amelioration and progress of mankind. Not only with reference to the question of religion, but also in respect of the political and social aspect of the present time, and of the distant future, however dark the clouds gathering around might appear, he still was sanguine and hopeful of brighter days. Of all the poems he wrote about this period, there is none more perfect, none more inspired with the true genius of poetry, than the following verses, setting forth this wise and prophetic hopefulness :—

    ' Say not, the struggle nought availeth,
      The labour and the wounds are vain,

The enemy faints not, nor faileth,
  And as things have been they remain.

If hopes were dupes, fears may be liars ;
  It may be, in yon smoke concealed,
Your comrades chase e'en now the fliers,
  And, but for you, possess the field.

For while the tired waves, vainly breaking,
  Seem here no painful inch to gain,
Far back, through creeks and inlets making,
  Comes silent, flooding in, the main.

And not by eastern windows only,
  When daylight comes, comes in the light,
In front the sun climbs slow, how slowly,
  But westward, look, the land is bright.'

There is, perhaps, no poem of equal brevity in the English language that gives us more pleasure than do these four short and simple stanzas, and after reading them once more, we feel the truth of the observations of Professor Masson, who writes, ' These poems of Clough have such merits of thought and expression, that were the volume torn up, and the anonymous leaves scattered here and there in Australia or Western America, or wherever afar off the English language is spreading, there would be some, doubtless, whom the fragments would arrest, and who would con them and repeat them as fine things by some unknown author.'

P

It was during the time of his residence in Gordon Square, that Clough, in the autumn of 1850, took advantage of his vacation and proceeded on a holiday expedition to Venice. The poem by which his fame is raised to its highest position among the poets of this century—the poem of *Dipsychus*—was begun during this journey, this visit to the 'white swan of cities,' as Longfellow poetically describes that northern capital of Italy. To this poem the next chapter is devoted ; it need not, therefore, be further referred to at present. About two years now passed by without any change, or marked event, taking place in the poet's mode of life. He lived quietly and soberly in that large red-brick building which still exists as University Hall, close to the Irvingite Church ;—he taught his pupils, and visited his not very numerous friends and acquaintances, and, as he tells us in the lines entitled, *In a London Square*, waited the advent of some more propitious condition of affairs. There are some persons who are by nature discontented, and, as it were, always dissatisfied with their own life and fortune, their environments, their business, their companions, and, indeed, with everything that is theirs. For them the world requires re-making

before it can be considered endurable, and whatever else may be uncertain (to slightly alter Pope's
well-known line)—

  'One truth is clear, whatever is, is *wrong !* '

Clough was not one of these.   He took the world
as he found it, and made the best of it, and could,
in a fashion of his own, even find a blessing in
being placed amongst uncongenial people.   He
made the best of life, even of the somewhat dull life
in Gordon Square, and was content with the work
and practical duties of daily toil and teaching which
it imposed.   ' Lay not your hand,' he writes at this
time, ' upon the veil of the inner sanctuary, to try and
lift it up ; go, thou proselyte of the gate, and do thy
service where it is permitted thee.   Is it for nothing,
but for the foolish souls of men to be discontented
and repine and whimper at, that He made this very
tolerably beautiful earth, with its logic and its
arithmetic, and its exact and punctual multifarious
arrangements, &c. &c. ?   Is it the end and object
of all finite creation that sentimental human sim-
pletons may whine about their infinite longings ?
Was it ordered that twice two should make four,
simply for the intent that boys and girls should be

cut to the heart that they do not make five? Be content, when the veil is raised, perhaps they will make five! who knows?'

At the beginning of 1852, when Clough had been about two years at University Hall, a college was founded at Sydney, and he decided at once upon offering himself as a candidate for the post of Principal of this new establishment. What induced him to take this step is not quite clear, but the probility would seem to be that he found his present employment not sufficiently remunerative, while that for which he now offered himself, would, we are told, have brought him a safe income, and one on which he could afford to marry. He was, at this time, it should be mentioned, already a lover, and, encouraged by the immediate prospect of obtaining this post at Sydney, he ventured to become engaged to the object of his attachment, Blanche, daughter of William Smith, Esq., of Combe Hurst, Surrey. Unfortunately he was, so far as the Sydney project was concerned, doomed to disappointment, for the post was given to Dr. Wooley; and Clough, who had, in consequence of this project, relinquished University Hall, once more found himself entirely without employment. An attempt to obtain an ap-

pointment in the Education Department at Whitehall also failed, owing to a change in the Government, and the downfall of the Liberal Ministry.
His position at this time was by no means satisfactory, and not seeing any possibility of procuring
a livelihood in England, he determined to cross the
Atlantic and try his fortune in America, where, as a
tutor and literary man, he felt confident of obtaining
remunerative work.　He was, moreover, encouraged
in this undertaking by his American friend Emerson, and hence, at the end of October, in 1852, he
sailed for America on board H.M.S. " Canada,"—
amongst his fellow-voyagers being Thackeray and
Lowell.　And here, for the present, we must leave
him while we discuss his two poems, *Dipsychus* and
Amours de Voyage, both of which had already been
written, although they were not published for many
years afterwards—in fact the former was not published in its entirety until eight years after his
death.

Chapter VII.

DIPSYCHUS.

THE 'Man of Two Souls,' for such is the meaning of the word, is not, perhaps, a very uncommon character. Mr. Tennyson, in his *Two
Voices*, has furnished us with a picture of a man of
this description, and has portrayed the wavering,
undecided mind or will (the *Ego* of the meta-
physicians), listening to its two spiritual counsellors
as they tender their discordant advice. Moreover,
to those whose intellects are of the subjective order,
it will be no new thing to be told that there is ' the
soul within the soul.' To such persons the privilege
is accorded of occasionally drawing aside the curtain,
and peeping quietly into the secluded inner chamber,
where they behold their ' other self' (*l'autre*, as it
has been called), sitting and thinking, willing, pondering, and considering. Hartley Coleridge, in
whom this subjective, or introspective, faculty was

largely developed, made the quaint discovery, while
he was yet a child, that he was not one, but several
Hartleys :—and when he was remonstrated with for
taking his pleasure too gravely, 'The pity is,' he
naïvely replied, 'the pity is, *I'se* always thinking of
my thoughts!'

It is to this not always very profitable employment, this 'thinking about our thoughts,' that we
are indebted for much of our clearest insight into
human nature. It is the fashion of some dramatists
and writers of fiction to portray their heroes as
faultless, their saints as spotless examples of un-
alloyed virtue, and their sinners as wholly wicked ;
and even in real life persons are too often inclined
to regard those whom they only know by public
report in somewhat the same extravagant fashion.
But such persons, such Monophysites, are either
wholly ignorant or somewhat forgetful of the fact
that human nature is more or less of a hotchpotch, a
mixture of good and evil ; and that the nature of
every one has some proportion of each, some ad-
mixture of Good, some alloy of Evil. The character of Jacob, as depicted in the Bible, is a typical
instance of this piebald spirituality, this twofold
nature of the human character. The chosen ser-

vant of the Lord, Israel, who 'as a prince hadst power with God and with men,' as we are told in the thirty-second chapter of Genesis, is also that Jacob who lied to Isaac, his father, and deprived his brother of the birthright and blessing to which he was justly entitled. The conflict between good and evil in Jacob was a conflict between the two opposed forces of the man's own nature; but in Clough's poem of *Dipsychus*, the conflict is rather between the tender conscience of Dipsychus on the one hand, and the World on the other, the latter being represented by the Spirit who throughout the poem holds converse with Dipsychus. This Spirit is, however, more or less of a mystery, and the poet evidently intended that such should be the case. The first hasty conclusion one arrives at respecting him is that he represents the more worldly of the two souls of Dipsychus, and this is not altogether incongruous with the information supplied respecting him in the various portions of the dialogue. He is put forward as a 'compound of convention and impiety,' and is at times even addressed by the titles of Mephistopheles and Belial. When he is himself asked to state his name, he retorts in his usual flippant and worldly fashion—

—— 'take your pick ; I've got a score—
Never a royal baby more.
For a brass plate upon a door
What think you of *Cosmocrator ?* '

'The Power of this World,' as opposed to the
higher principles, and purer, holier yearnings of a
noble and true heart, is doubtless the best definition
that can be given of this so-called *Spirit*. If we
compare him with the character of *Mephistopheles*,
as depicted by Goethe, in *Faust*, we perceive that
they are altogether dissimilar, for the latter is
plainly and entirely the spirit of evil, although a
learned spirit withal, whereas Clough's is a much
more subtle creation, corresponding more closely
with the character of what is usually termed a ' man
of the world' than with that of the legendary Prince
of Darkness. The Spirit himself, in one portion of
the poem, with much *amour propre*, sarcastically
observes—

' One wouldn't like, even if a true devil,
To be taken for a vulgar Jew devil.'

And in the prose Epilogue appended to the poem
this view of the Spirit's personality is more or less
confirmed, as in the following excerpt :—

'I don't very well understand what it's all about,' said my uncle; 'but there was a great deal that was unmeaning, vague, and involved; and what was most plain, was least decent and least moral.'

'Dear sir,' said I, 'says the proverb, 'Needs must when the devil drives;' and if the devil is to speak ——'

'Well,' said my uncle, 'why should he? Nobody asked him. Not that he didn't say much which, if only it hadn't been for the way he said it, and that it was he who said it, would have been sensible enough.'

'But sir,' said I, 'perhaps he wasn't a devil after all.'

It is, indeed, not improbable that, if instead of designating the two *dramatis personæ* in his poem, *Dipsychus* and the *Spirit*, Clough had given them some other names or titles that conveyed no meaning—say, for instance, Dipsychus had been called *Damon*, and the Spirit had been simply *Rinaldo*—many readers would have been of the opinion that the latter was by far the finer and wiser fellow of the two, especially when the Spirit observes—

> 'Like a good subject and wise man,
> Believe whatever things you can.
> Take your religion as 'twas found you,
> And say no more of it, confound you !'

The poem of *Easter Day*, which precedes that of *Dipsychus*, should, we think, be read as an introductory prologue to the latter. It was composed at Naples, in which town the juxtaposition of religion and the grosser forms of immorality is especially remarkable. Catholicism, with its numerous crucifixes, its attractive services, and its ecclesiastical decorations, is presented to the view of the beholder, amid a world of unparalleled wickedness and depravity :—the banner of the Roman Church has been floating for centuries over what can only be described as a 'sink of iniquity.' It is impossible for those that are serious and in earnest about religious matters, not to perceive and accept the lesson which the sights and social aspects of such a town plainly inculcate, namely, the lesson that Christianity, as there taught and practised, is a complete failure. To Clough, who had witnessed the godly character and goodly living of a man like Dr. Arnold, who had in him beheld the righteous fruit of a reasonable faith, and had so often heard him denounce the errors and follies of Ritualism and Romanism, this lesson must have, indeed, been one of terrible and irresistible force. And so this poem of *Easter Day*, this lava stream of irrepressible emotion, this torrid production of grief and despair, plainly indicates that it was. ' Is this,' we can in imagination hear him exclaiming, ' is this the result of so many centuries of so-called Christian teaching ? Is this the result for which Christ suffered, and was buried, and rose again on that first Easter morning ?' How impressive are the lines with which the poem opens, how solemn, forcible, and devout,—

> ' Through the great sinful streets of Naples as I past,
>   With fiercer heat than flamed above my head
> My heart was hot within me ; till at last
>   My brain was lightened when my tongue had said—
>   Christ is not risen !'

  *   *   *   *

And again—

>   'Ashes to ashes, dust to dust ;
>   As of the unjust, also of the just—
>   Yea, of that Just One, too !
>   This is the one sad gospel that is true—
>   Christ is not risen !
>   Is He not risen, and shall we not rise ?
>   Oh, we unwise !'

Such are the thoughts, the fears, and misgivings which are suggested and aroused in the poet's mind by the apparent impotence of the Church of Rome to rescue from sin and debauchery the inhabitants of a town renowned for its profligacy. But these fears and misgivings are, in a measure, cast aside, if, indeed, they are not completely met and answered, in the concluding portion of the prologue, and as the poet turns his back upon Naples, hope once more takes the place of despondence, and the prologue concludes with the words—

> ' He is yet risen indeed ;
> Christ is yet risen.'

In *Dipsychus* the scene is changed to the Piazza at Venice, and a year has elapsed since the preceding lines were written. The Spirit is present with Dipsychus, answering his lamentations, and longings for a nobler life with the mocking flippancy of the world. As in the Toledo at Naples, so again now at Venice, Dipsychus is impressed with the apparent practical failure of the attempt to impart a higher spirituality—

> ' Where people, true enough, appear
> To appreciate more and understand
> Their ices, and their Austrian band,
> And dark-eyed girls ——'

Once more he exclaims ' Christ is not risen,' but the Spirit is now at hand ; the ' persecuting voice that haunts him,' whispers in his ear that he should do as others do, that he should relinquish these too highly-conscientious questionings, these superfine views respecting Duty and Religion, and should enjoy the good things of this world;—Life, he hints, little loves such peevish piety, it is not well to be behind your fellow-men in such matters, feast on the sweets, enjoy the present, these ices, *par exemple*, and the *dolce far niente*, the company and the evening air.

> ' Up, to the caffé ! take a chair,
> And join the wiser idlers there.
> And see that fellow singing yonder ;
> Singing, ye gods, and dancing too—
> Tooraloo, tooraloo, tooraloo loo—
> Fiddledi, diddledi, diddle di di ;
> Figaro sù, Figaro giù—
> Figaro quà, Figaro là !
> How he likes doing it—Ha, ha !'

But the heart of Dipsychus is not so easily led away captive, nor does he cease to commune with himself respecting his holier aspirations, his higher ideals, and yearnings towards a severer purity of thought and action. Before his gaze was the crowd, coming and going;—the vanities and follies—the parade of human passion in its heedless pursuit of pleasure, these his eyes beheld; but how different the scenes of which he had read, the scenes of old, cherished and remembered, and referred to by him

in some of his poems, in *Easter Day*, for instance,
in the lines—

> Weep not beside His tomb,
> Ye women unto whom
> He was great comfort and yet greater grief ;
> Nor ye, ye faithful few, that wont with Him to roam,
> Seek sadly what for Him ye left, go hopeless to your home.

How is the spectacle before him to be brought
into harmony with the teaching of the Gospel?
how is the conduct of the Christians of the present
time to be reconciled with the belief which they
profess in the doctrines and tenets of their Church?
Did the facts related in the New Testament really
take place to bring about such results as these?
These are the questions that the poet suggests as
present in the mind of Dipsychus, not indeed stated
in so many words, yet conveyed not the less clearly
under the transparent veil of the poetic medium,—
as Dipsychus, gazing at the crowd before him,
exclaims—

> 'The Campanile to the silent stars
> Goes up, above—its apex lost in air—
> While these do what?'
>> 'Ah, heaven! too true, at Venice
> Christ is not risen either.'

In the second scene they have passed from the

Piazza to the Public Gardens, and here it may be pointed out that this, the second scene, is perhaps the least interesting portion of the Dialogue. But in poetry of this description it is necessary to have what may be termed 'resting-places,' where the mind of the reader, as well as that of the poet, may be prepared for pages of greater brilliancy; and moreover there is a *chiaro-oscuro* in poetry as in painting, which requires the author to be not unmindful of the judicious arrangement of the light and shade, on which the effect of the picture so greatly depends. It is the undulation produced by valley and mountain, and not the high level of the table-land, that furnishes the finest and most picturesque scenery, and it is occasionally well to descend even into the tranquil Valley of Dulness in order to more thoroughly appreciate the lofty peaks and towering summits of poetic genius that stand on either side. The scene in the Public Gardens does not glitter with the rich crystals of wit and repartee,—does not sparkle with the flashes of light and wisdom,—that are so noticeable in other portions of the poem, yet it serves, no doubt, the purpose for which it was intended, as indicated in the above remarks.

From the public gardens Dipsychus returns to
the hotel, and here the Spirit urges upon him the
advisability of acquiescing in the conventional ways
of the world, putting forward the claims and advantages of Society, and recommending that with
his assistance he should turn his attention to the
subject of matrimony, with a view to making what
is usually termed a 'good match';—'and,' continues
Mephistopheles,—

> ' With sagacity
> Much might be done by one of your capacity.
> A virtuous attachment formed judiciously
> Would come, one sees, uncommonly propitiously :
> Turn you but your affections the right way,
> And what mayn't happen none of us can say,
> For, in despite of devils and of mothers,
> Your good young men make catches, too, like others.'

In these lines, which are hardly as rhythmical as
they might be, one has a good illustration of the
resemblance which some writers have discovered
between the satirical vein in Clough's character and
the more bitter irony of Byron.   But although the
lines which we have just quoted, especially the final
couplet, have, it is true, a decidedly Byronic flavour,
yet if one compares the two poets together throughout the whole of their compositions, the resem-

blance is found to be much like that between
Macedon and Monmouth; there is a river in Macedon and there is a river in Monmouth, and there
the similarity ends. But Byron is not the only
poet to whom Clough is alleged to be somewhat
similar. He has the strange privilege (in the
opinions of different writers) of resembling not
only Byron, but also Chaucer, Crabbe, Wordsworth,
Heinrich Heine, Burns, Goethe, Béranger, and even
Alfred de Musset,—not to mention the classic
poets, Homer and Lucretius. And yet no one has
ever questioned the distinct individuality and originality of Clough's poems. It is the old story of
the chameleon; you may declare that it is green,
or affirm that it is blue, yet it is still the chameleon, and these different colours that you notice are
but the variable effects of variable causes, and of
the light in which you behold it.

To return, however, to Dipsychus, and the
Spirit's sagacious pleading on behalf of Society,
with its various advantages, its polish and refined
manners, its 'ingenuous graces' no less than its
courteous insincerity, its union of the serpent and
the dove,—the Spirit urges 'what we all love is
good touched up with evil,' and he adds—

'Good manners,' said our great-aunts, 'next to piety :
And so, my friend, hurrah for good society !'

Again Dipsychus remains not convinced, and
refuses to be persuaded by his worldly counsellor.
He declines, as he puts it, with perhaps unnecessary severity, to 'drain the heart with endless
complaisance,' to 'twist the mouth to counterfeit,'
to forestall the spontaneity of the heart with
'pallid hotbed courtesies ';—and he exclaims with
passionate fervour that to do these things, however
diplomatic, would indeed be to 'lose one's youth
too early.' To which the Spirit promptly replies,

'*Du tout!*
To give up nature's just what would not do.'

The next scene brings us once more to the
Piazza, and here, by some accidental misapprehen-
sion, a Croat or German officer threatens and so
insults the absent-minded, meditative Dipsychus,
who, to the Spirit's surprise and disgust, does not,
however, proceed to demand satisfaction or otherwise punish the offender. 'It was a mistake, he is
wrong, but let him go ! I'll not pollute my fingers
by picking up the fallen coin of honour from the
dirt.' So he argues with his indignant counsellor,

but the latter is for once thoroughly aroused, and he exclaims with disdain, 'You, well-bred, well-born, to behave thus, as though you had been some shopkeeper's son and knew naught better than bills of creditor and debtor! to be threatened by a beast like that! Do you know that '*fort*' means '*get out*'? But let us leave Italy, and go to the 'great peace-meeting' up at Frankfort—

> ' To the Peace Congress ! ring the bell !
> Horses to Frankfort and to ——'

But Dipsychus confesses that he is not quite in union with himself on this matter, and it is a question on which there is much difference of opinion whether it is right or moral to encourage tyranny, violence, or injustice, by allowing it to go unpunished. To persons of a quiet nature, who love to pursue their 'peaceful byway walk,' it is no doubt a hard and uncongenial task, to return blow for blow,—we do not mean out of revenge, but simply to teach the offender that he cannot do wrong with impunity, and so prevent his repeating the offence upon other persons. *De minimis non curat lex*, and there are a thousand methods in which legal cruelty and injustice can be

committed, and for which there is but one remedy,
namely, that suggested by the 'equities of self-
defence.' The advice given by Polonius to Laertes
has been repeated by many a Christian gentleman
when sending his son to a public school in some such
words as these :—' Do not be quarrelsome my boy,
or cantankerous, but if any fellow does attack you,
hit back, and *hard!*' Thus far would we endorse
the gospel of giving a 'Rowland for an Oliver;' but
on the other hand, one must not forget that in dealing
with others, especially with those who are beneath
us in rank and education, there is always room for
generosity and forbearance, for charity and consideration, and that a readiness to forgive is as much
the quality of a gentleman as the repression of
offence. The whole of this portion of the dialogue
is admirably written, and leaves little room for fault-
finding, but it is not improbable that if the poem
had been published in Clough's life-time he would
have made some slight verbal alterations, and would
not, for instance, have allowed two successive lines
to have ended with the same word, ' myself,'—but
these are small matters, and detract but little from
the general excellence of the poem.

The last scene of the First Part is on the Lido,

the place where Byron used to ride, and here the colloquy assumes a more sombre character, while Dipsychus relates to the Spirit how, during the hours of darkness, he had dreamt a dream in which he had heard a bell sounding all the night, tinkling and tinkling, then tolling, then tinkling, then tolling again. A mingling of mirth and of woe! The tinkling of gaiety, of shallow light-hearted revellers, who, while accepting the hypothesis that there is no Supreme Ruler of the universe, go on their way indifferent, or even foolishly rejoicing in their newly discovered freedom from restraint:—and on the other hand, the tolling of woe in the hearts of the wise, the mourning and weeping in the house of the soul that yearns for the peace that dwells alone with those whose faith is assured ; the tolling of the everlasting hope that longs to believe, and is told that its belief is a delusion. Dipsychus, in relating his dream, gives utterance to both these views, but they are not put forward as his own, still less as being those of the poet himself. They are simply portions of a dark and dreadful dream that only departed when, like a good angel, through the white curtains of his bed, the light of morning came in and touched him.

The Spirit, it is needless to state, is in no way backward in setting forth his own especial tenets and opinions on a subject in which he is so particularly interested ; and as soon as Dipsychus has told his story he at once takes up the theme, and presently introduces a short poem of his own, respecting which a living author, and member of Parliament at the present time, has observed that it is one of the most perfect little pieces that ever were written, and that Heine himself has done nothing more terse, or more *spirituel.* In order that the reader may judge for himself how far this high praise is deserved, we quote the following verses :—

> ' There is no God,' the wicked saith,
> ' And truly it 's a blessing,
> For what He might have done with us
> It's better only guessing.'

> *   *   *   *   *

> ' There is no God, or if there is,'
> The tradesman thinks, ' 'twere funny
> If he should take it ill in me
> To make a little money.'

> *   *   *   *   *

> ' Some others, also, to themselves,
> Who scarce so much as doubt it,

Think there is none, when they are well,
    And do not think about it.

' But country folks who live beneath
    The shadow of the steeple ;
The parson and the parson's wife,
    And mostly married people ;

' Youths green and happy in first love,
    So thankful for illusion ;
And men caught out in what the world
    Calls guilt, in first confusion ;

' And almost every one when age,
    Disease, or sorrows strike him,
Inclines to think there is a God,
    Or something very like Him.'

From the Lido the scene changes to the interior arcade of the Doge's Palace, where they take shelter from a storm, and where the Spirit avails himself of the opportunity to lecture Dipsychus, in his own fashion, on his want of clearness and steadfastness. Referring to his poem of *Easter-Day*, he urges that it is anything but plain what is the intention or meaning of the lines, though, he adds, the tone is clearly ironical,—

    ' Sarcastic, say ; or were it fitter
    To style it the religious bitter ? '

This want of explicitness, this continual change of front, this practice of taking opposite views of the same question, is what to many persons, besides this spirit of various titles, will appear to be the weakest part of Clough's poem. It is, or it may seem, unsatisfactory to be told that the same thing is both black and white ; the majority of mankind are agreed either that the thing is as white as the snow on the side of the mountain, or otherwise they have decided, and are 'as certain as they are of their own existence,' that the thing is black. 'Either it is black, or it is white,' others will say, 'but please do not add to our difficulty, do not make 'confusion worse confounded,' by telling us first that it is one, and then as plainly intimating that it is the other.' But unfortunately truth always has *at least* two sides to it, and sometimes half-a-dozen :—it is always both black and white at the same time in the judgments of two different persons, while it is by no means improbable that a third will gravely shake his head, exclaiming ' οὐδὲ τόδε οὐδὲ τἄλλο,—it is neither black, nor yet white !' Moreover, it is the more shallow and short-sighted minds that are the quickest to form a judgment on all subjects ; and that are fully convinced, or (to again use Cardinal

Newman's expression) 'as certain as they are of
their own existence,' that there are, or are not,
living organisms in Saturn or Sirius, or in the wonderful comet of 1680. Other minds, on the contrary, are not so gifted, and are simply content to
acknowledge that on all questions of 'lunar politics'
they are unable to form a judgment. Clough was
one of these, and in his case the words 'lunar
politics' included many dogmas, and doctrines,
many points of social and religious uncertainty,
which the world at large has settled in a rough and
ready fashion of its own, for without having verified its premises, it has hastily completed the
syllogism by writing down the conclusion. The
author of *Dipsychus* differed from other people in
that he was not so eager about completing the
syllogism, as he was of verifying the premises, and
examining the data. He was always afraid (to
quote his own words) of 'adding up too soon,'
before all the figures were before him, and before
the sum was, in very truth, complete. Professor
Huxley, in one of his *Lay Sermons*, has told us that
'the man of science has learned to believe in justifi-
cation not by faith, but by verification;'—and this
appears to have also been the case with Clough. Yet

he was not desirous to destroy the edifice which the thought and labour of past ages had built and consecrated. It has been observed, with much truth, that in parting from the existing theology, he made no attempt to turn again and rend it, and that he remained singularly tolerant and courteous in his relations to those with whom he no longer agreed. The line,

> ' Whom God deludes is well deluded,'

occurs in *Dipsychus*, and it shows that his views were not those of the iconoclast, but of the simple and reverent seeker after truth.

But to return to the subject of the poem,—the following scene finds the two disputants in a gondola on the Grand Canal, and Dipsychus appears for once to be happy and contented. As they glide along, quietly and smoothly, past now some palace front, and now a passing bark, he is at last delighted, and exclaims with ecstasy,—

> ' How light we move, how softly ! Ah,
> Were life but as the gondola !'

The local colouring given to the poem is noticeable in this and other portions of *Dipsychus*. As in the *Bothie* we had the marked manners, customs, and scenery of the Highlands ;—so now the poet gives us Venice with all its characteristic phases, its shadowy canals, its 'untrodden streets' (as another writer poetically describes them), its piazzas, spires, public gardens, and gondolas. Clough never attempted to write of the far distant Past, or of places that he had not seen, but he was most fortunate in choosing for his principal poems the two countries, so different from each other, which are nevertheless especially suited for the purposes of poetry. It were no exaggeration to say that Italy and Scotland are in themselves soul-stirring, beautiful poems. The gentle movement of the gondola is peculiar to Venice and its ocean-streams,—the sunny sky and the cadence of musical words and love-impassioned language is characteristic of the whole of Italy. Dipsychus is, as we have said, delighted with the easy gliding over the peaceful, moonlit water, and his only cause for regret is the thought that for their pleasure the wretched gondolier is toiling at the oar. 'To make,' he exclaims in sorrow, 'to make one's fellow-man an instrument'—'Is,' the Spirit smartly retorts, 'just the thing that makes him most content.' This, which may be called the 'Gondola Scene,' is, on the whole, well written, but we must take exception to the

rhyming hexameters here introduced in the dialogue, which are as bad as rhyming hexameters
must inevitably be. On the other hand it will be
noticed that Clough has throughout the poem
shown admirable skill and judgment in setting the
worldly wisdom and observations of the Spirit to a
jingling vulgar metre, while the nobler thoughts
and holier aspirations of Dipsychus are expressed
in the pathetic language and rhythm of true poetry.
This difference of diction and rhythm is especially
noticeable in two poems which occur at this point,
and of which we quote the opening stanzas in illustration of the above remarks. In the one we have
Dipsychus speaking, in solemn earnestness, the
exquisite lines,—

> ' O let me love my love unto myself alone,
> And know my knowledge to the world unknown ;
> No witness to the vision call,
> Beholding, unbeheld of all ;
> And worship thee, with thee withdrawn, apart,
> Whoe'er, whate'er thou art,
> Within the closest veil of mine own inmost heart.'

*　　*　　*　　*　　*

In the other we have the jeering spirit of this world
giving utterance to the wisdom of the wealthy
parvenu who ' lords it ' over the poorer classes,—

'As I sat at the café, I said to myself,
They may talk as they please about what they call pelf,
They may sneer as they like about eating and drinking,
But help it I cannot, I cannot help thinking,
    How pleasant it is to have money, heigh ho !
    How pleasant it is to have money.'

      *   *   *   *   *

The latter poem is a striking picture of the most unpleasant description of the ' man of the world,'— the Dives of mushroom growth, destitute alike of feeling and of education, to whom years of money-making and labour-cheapening, has given a heart of stone and the brain of a calculating-machine. Clough does not hesitate to paint his portrait in its most significant and disagreeable outlines, and with a plainness and daring that would do credit to Hogarth. The new millionaire boastfully relates how he drives through the streets with all the people staring at his grandeur, while if he 'should chance to run over a cad,' he is always able to 'pay for the damage if ever so bad.'   In the evening he goes to the theatre or the opera,—

'We stroll to our box and look down on the pit,
And if it weren't low should be tempted to spit ;
We loll and we talk until people look up,
And when it's half over we go out to sup.
    So pleasant it is to have money, heigh ho !
    So pleasant it is to have money.'

      *   *   *   *   *

To such an one we feel disposed to use the words of *Gil Blas*, and to wish him 'all sorts of prosperity with a little more taste.'

It is during a conversation in the Academy that Dipsychus first begins to show a weariness of mere dreaming and thinking, and his love of reflection and introspection is supplanted by a desire for action. He longs at last to relinquish the character of thinker and philosopher, and to become, if not a 'man of the world,' at any rate, a man of useful and heroic deeds. He summons Mephistopheles, the Spirit, who, 'like an eaves-dropping menial on his thought,' instantaneously answers his call,—and him he consults on the subject. To the question, what are the terms he demands for the world's merchandise? Mephistopheles replies, to his surprise and wonder, that he must go to church, or at the least take a pew 'to send his wife and servants to;' and further suggests that he should enter a profession, the Law or Holy Orders. But neither of these courses quite suits the inclinations of Dipsychus, and in the world's work he seems to behold little that is free from impurity, little that can be done without contamination and a loss of freedom and integrity. He once more dismisses

his counsellor, and in St. Mark's when he is again
alone, he pours forth in an eloquent soliloquy his
meditations on the 'vext conundrums of our life,'
and the best mode of securing noble action, and
not unworthy work;—not a mere treadmill, he
adds, nor a yielding to base mechanical adroitness.
But, in the end, he confesses that it is in the 'pell-
mell of men' that high deeds are found, and not by
the 'fringy edges of the fight,' and the conclusion
of his reflections points to a submission to the
demands of the Spirit of this World, and his final
words are—

'Adieu, ye twisted thinkings.　I submit : it must be.'

The same line of argument is carried on through
the remaining scenes which bring the dialogue to a
close.　Thus the poem of *Dipsychus* ends, and of
the unfinished fragment which follows, entitled
Dipsychus Continued, it is unnecessary for us to
offer any criticism, as it is manifestly so incomplete
as not to admit of any satisfactory treatment.

The analysis which we have given of this, the
most important of Clough's works, may appear
somewhat lengthy, but on turning to the poem
itself the reader will at once perceive that we have

only referred to the salient features, and that we have passed over many pages, and many brilliant passages, without either criticism or remark ; and that whole scenes, as for instance that ' At Torcello,' with the beautiful lyric beginning *When the enemy is near thee*, have been left entirely unnoticed, and have been permitted, as it were, to pass silently by unquestioned. But when we mention that Clough's poems cover four hundred and ninety-seven pages it will be easily understood that reference can only be made in a work of this description to those portions of his writings which appear to be of most value and of the highest interest.

Of *Dipsychus* in its entirety, we must confess that it is, when beheld in its present state, simply a *cul-de-sac ;*—or, if the reader prefer it, a suite of richly-adorned chambers, but not a perfect palace. If Clough had lived he might, like Goethe, have gradually, through a period of thirty years, developed his work, and at the age of sixty have delighted the world with the publication of another masterpiece,—another palace of art, or ' lordly pleasure-house' for the soul. But Death would not have it so. And what is, we would ask, the judgment of those who have studied, and publicly

R

criticized, this unique production of English literature,—more especially as compared with its great
German prototype.　Mr. Symonds writes respecting
it,—'the problems agitated by Clough are of a
more subtle and spiritual nature than those which
Goethe raised.　They are worked out with less
attention to artistic finish and dramatic effect than
the speculations which underlie the play of *Faust.*
In their narrow compass they strike many students
as being more forcible in thought and more full of
feeling than the meditative scenes of Goethe's
drama.　Clough was content to be wholly un-
dramatic and monotonous.　Instead of presenting
us with numerous highly-coloured pictures, he dis-
sected a portion of the troubled brain of one man
with marvellous skill and delicacy.　Thus the two
works are essentially different in their scope and
aim ; and the resemblance between them is superficial.'—And the following is the judgment of one
who is, perhaps, of all living authors, best qualified
to speak authoritatively respecting a poem of this
description :—'Fragment as it is, we think it deserves no meaner title than that of our " English
Faust."　Of the many writers who have been influenced by the great German, no one has so entirely

caught his spirit, no one has so happily succeeded in combining the grave and solemn with the light and ironical. It has been often remarked that we have no good translation of *Faust*, because, in the first place, the translator of *Faust* should be himself a poet; and in the next, this poet must be alike capable of the profound and the lively, the pensive and the satirical. Now this requisite combination we have here in *Dipsychus*. But we must not let it be understood for a moment that, because we allude to the influence of Goethe, the poem itself is one of an imitative character. If the fact that the materials are drawn entirely from the writer's own inner experience constitute originality, this is pre-eminently an original poem. It is the expression of the man himself, of various thoughts that, at different times, have come unbidden into his mind. And here let us at once make an observation which it is well to bear in mind in reading and appreciating this poem. It deals with great subjects, and these are treated from opposite points of view. But the subtleties, or the audacities of thought we meet with, are never cold inventions or elaborate ingenuities. We have no paradoxes designedly contrived to startle or to amuse. The subtlety or audacity of thought is always a genuine product of the thinker. There is a charming levity of manner in parts, but no great subject is really *played with*. Taken as a whole, it is the gravest of all colloquies a man could hold with himself.'

The writer whose words we have here quoted, has, we think, stated the merits of *Dipsychus* in a fair and appreciative spirit. 'It deals,' he states, 'with great subjects.' And what, we would ask, can be of more importance, or of more absorbing interest, to mankind, than such a 'criticism of life,' such a disquisition on the ways of the world, such an attempt to discover the rational rule of human conduct, as Clough puts before us in this poem. There are times when the accepted dogmas of historical religion are subject to change, when creeds that have long existed are openly questioned, discussed, and assailed, and it is well that at such seasons we should have the beauty of holiness, of purity, and nobility of character, put forward on its own basis apart from any question of church, sect, or belief. An enthusiastic writer, speaking of the disturbed state of Europe at the close of the last century, observes—'Ancient landmarks, covered with the moss of many years, were torn up. The guidance of principles, drawn not from any customary or conventional authority, but from the depths of human nature, was needed alike for those who hailed and those who abhorred the change. Men long accustomed to float on the placid waters of a river, within sight and reach of safe and smiling shores, found themselves suddenly driven out upon a stormy and shoreless sea, and, in their peril, some were earnestly gazing for a beacon-light from the lost coast, others were idly gazing at the flashing fires that crest the dark billows of the deep, and a few were looking upward hopefully for some star in the cloudy sky * * * * Ancient opinions and rules of life were abandoned, and new modes of thought and feeling took their place.'

It is at seasons and periods of disturbance such as are here referred to, that the religious element in literature is especially useful, provided it does not merely take the shape of superficial precepts, but deals with the larger sympathies and more complex principles of human nature. There are spiritual facts that do not and cannot change, and which are of lasting power and influence in shaping and moulding both character and conduct. The love of self, no less than the love of others ; the principle which underlies Calvinism as well as that which has prompted Universalism :—*egoism* as well as *altruism,*—are both capable of being conducive to the good of society, of civilization, and of human happiness. And in respect of these two qualities, these two attributes of man's nature, we are, each one of us, a veritable Dipsychus,—we are fashioned, that is to say, as though we had two separate and distinct souls. But if we pass from the individual to the social body, to any sect, society or nation, we shall still meet with the same two-fold principle of self-preservation and the desire to benefit mankind,—we shall still find mingled with worldliness, and the struggle for conquest, hopes and yearnings of a higher and holier nature. As, in the words of Dipsychus, we bear

> 'The workday burden of dull life
> About these footsore flags of a weary world,'

the spirit within us yearns for union with the purer existence ; we are eager to retire from the greed and money-winning chicanery of the mart, as well as from the vanities and vain strivings of society ; we are desirous of departing from what is small and

ignoble, no less than from what is impure or
unholy. Like Dipsychus we behold the clear stars
above us, on the 'roseate westward sky,' and we
fain would be absorbed into their essential purity
and be one with them. Or again, we see the great
mountains wrapping their heads in the solemn
clouds, so sternly lifted above our human conten-
tions and frivolities, and we become wishful to
share their solemn grandeur, and put away from us
the petty pursuits of this narrow, noisy world,—
these matters

> 'too small
> For any record on the leaves of time:'—

and these aspirations, these vague dreams and holy
longings, are not fruitless or without effect, although
they may often yield to the demands of our daily
existence and the prosaic necessities of life. We
descend from these flights of the spirit, and return
once more to the things of this world, but we tread
the earth with a surer step, and value the 'positive
and present' more correctly, for having for a time
moved in a higher and clearer atmosphere. Lord
Byron in *Manfred* refers to this subject in the
following lines, but the views put forward are

characteristically different from those of *Dipsy-chus.*

> —' Beautiful !
> How beautiful is all this visible world !
> How glorious in its action and itself !
> But we, who name ourselves its sovereigns, we,
> Half dust, half deity, alike unfit
> To sink or soar, with our mix'd essence make
> A conflict of its elements, and breathe
> The breath of degradation and of pride,
> Contending with low wants and lofty will,
> Till our mortality predominates,
> And men are—what they name not to themselves,
> And trust not to each other.'

It is perhaps with this poem of Byron's that Clough's *Dipsychus* can most properly be compared, and not with perfect dramas such as *Faust* and *Hamlet*, though there may be some slight kinship, or similarity, between the four heroic metaphysical characters depicted in these poems. *Manfred* is practically a monologue,—*Dipsychus* is a colloquy between the two inner spiritual voices of one and the same man :—both poems are relieved by the introduction of lyrics of rare beauty, those in *Man-fred* being some of the finest that Byron ever wrote. The hero, however, of Lord Byron's poem is one tortured by the remembrance of his own past sins,—a criminal, who when the Evil One summons him to the lower world, promptly retorts with scorn,—

> ' I have not been thy dupe, nor am thy prey—
> But was my own destroyer, and will be
> My own hereafter.'—

Clough's hero, on the contrary, is one whose over-tender conscience cannot accept the conventional standard of every-day duty, or the worldly doctrines and counterfeit practices of modern life.

There is, moreover, a more important difference between the two characters of Manfred and Dipsychus, and it is one which distinguishes, and is applicable to, nearly all the compositions of these two poets. We refer to the fact that whereas Manfred is the fabulous hero of romance, somewhat terrible, strained, and unreal,—Dipsychus is plainly human —a character both possible and probable. Mr. Hutton, in comparing Clough to Goethe, has pointed out that he has ' the same love of homely naturalness of manner, of the wholesome flavour of earth, an even deeper desire to tame or exorcise all romance that is alien to common sense, and the same intellectual disposition to give common sense the casting vote, wherever there seems to be a conflict between it and the thirst of his own nature for something deeper.' This unwillingness to offend against common sense, or against probability, is a quality which may possibly become more general as the progress of science more plainly demonstrates the omnipresent reign of law, and gradually diminishes the domain of the supernatural or miraculous. Only in the stories for children shall we, perhaps, find ere long the extravagantly depicted paragon, the marvellous hero of fiction, or the terrible and wicked demigod of our sensational three-volumed novels. Clough has, we think, in this respect shown his good sense in making his *Mephistopheles*, or *Spirit*, no infernal visitant from the so-called ' lower regions,' (wherever they may be,) but a personification of the thoughts and feelings of the man himself who is tempted by the life and world around him, in precisely the same manner as any living organism may be influenced, either for its own good or otherwise, by its environments acting in conjunction with its own inner nature. As *Manfred* exclaims in the lines quoted above, ' I was my own destroyer,'—so all men who have come to spiritual destruction, must acknowledge that they have been to a great extent their own destroyers, and it is but childish folly, of which every intelligent man ought by this time to be thoroughly and heartily ashamed, to invent an Evil Spirit, or hobgoblin of wickedness, and make it a kind of scapegoat for our mis-doings. The Duke of Argyll in his work on *The Reign of Law*, has put the question, 'Can it be helpful or useful to believe a lie?'—and we have no hesitation in replying in the negative so far as the existence of this evilly-disposed monster is concerned, who is supposed to bear such spite against the human race that he is always tempting them to their own destruction. Alas! that there should be a similarity, however slight, between our arch-enemy, Beelzebub, and that strange being, the *Watermamma*, which throughout the whole of Guiana is said to take a demoniacal delight in waylaying and destroying travellers:—'There are,' writes the naturalist, Waterton, 'dreadful stories told concerning a horrible beast called the *Watermamma*, which, when it happens to take a spite against a canoe, rises out of the river, and in the most unrelenting manner possible carries both canoe and occupants down to the bottom with it, and then destroys them. Ludicrous extravagances! pleasing to those fond of the marvellous, and excellent matter for a distempered brain.'

Chapter VIII.

AMOURS DE VOYAGE,

AND

MARI MAGNO.

THE two most striking and important poems that Clough has left us are, in the opinion of the majority, *Dipsychus* and the *Bothie*, but there are a few critics who apparently do not concur in this judgment. One of these has observed that the '*Amours de Voyage* is, perhaps, the most highly finished, various, and artistically complete of all his works.' For our own part we should rather apply these words to the *Bothie*, and our opinion appears to be confirmed by the fact that whenever we mention Clough's name to strangers we usually find that they at once proceed to extol with enthusiasm the beauty, the humour, the pathos, and the various other excellences of his 'Long-Vacation Pastoral.'

Yet if we acknowledge that the *Bothie* is Clough's *Evangeline*, to the *Amours de Voyage* must be allotted the place occupied amongst Longfellow's poems by that poet's *Courtship of Miles Standish*. And it may here be observed that this last-mentioned poem was written after Longfellow had perused the *Bothie*, but the hexameters, although more perfect than those in the *Evangeline*, do not bear much metrical resemblance to Clough's spondaic and more compact lines. It is, however, divided like the *Bothie* into nine books, or parts, whereas *Evangeline* does not follow the example set by Goethe's *Hermann and Dorothea* in this respect, but is concluded in five cantos.

The *Amours de Voyage* was written in the year after that in which the *Bothie* was composed ; but while the latter was published within a month of its composition, the *Amours* did not see the light until no fewer than nine long years had elapsed, and was then only published apologetically in an American magazine, the *Atlantic Monthly*. Clough doubted of its execution, which he thought did not do justice to the conception, but he appears to have sent the poem to a friend soon after it was written, and the criticism he received seems to have some-

what displeased him, and we suspect that this unfavourable criticism by a 'candid friend' was the
cause of so fine a poem remaining unpublished for
so many years.   Moreover he was not assured as
regards the manner in which it would be received
by the committee ruling the affairs of University
Hall, of which he was at this time Principal.

In one respect this poem is indeed unique, for it
was composed while the author was shut up in
Rome during the time when that city was besieged
by the French in 1849.   The Roman citizens under
Mazzini had formed themselves into a little republic, and the French Government had sent an army
under General Oudinot, and after publishing a pro-
clamation which deceived the Italians and procured
for them a friendly reception, had eventually proceeded to bombard Rome.   It was during this
period that the *Amours de Voyage* was written, as we
are told in the following elegiac lines which form
the Epilogue to the poem :—

' So go forth to the world, to the good report and the evil !
   Go, little book ! thy tale, is it not evil and good ?
Go, and if strangers revile, pass quietly by without answer.
   Go, and if curious friends ask of thy rearing and age,
Say, ' I am flitting about many years from brain unto brain of
   Feeble and restless youths born to inglorious days :

But,' so finish the word, 'I was writ in a Roman chamber,
When from Janiculan heights thundered the cannon of
France.'

This bombardment of Rome by the French is so
closely connected, and is, as it were, so interwoven
with the thread of the poet's story, that it is necessary to remind the reader of the events which had
led up to so strange a spectacle as that of one
Republic attacking another with a view to restoring
the despotism which the latter had for the moment
succeeded in casting off. These events are clearly
narrated in a speech made by Lord Beaumont in
the House of Lords, on the 14th May, 1849, in which
he stated that the misgovernment of the Roman
territory, under the rule of successive Popes, had
brought about such a condition of the country that
nothing but the strong hand of a stronger power
could prevent the people rising in insurrection. On
the succession of Pius the Ninth the question arose
whether the policy of his predecessors should be
continued or modified, and to prevent outbreak the
latter course was adopted. But in carrying out
this decision fresh difficulties occurred, and an
attempt was made to separate the Pope's temporal
and spiritual powers by the appointment of lay

councillors with a sacerdotal government. The
Roman people were not satisfied with this, and
demanded the same liberty which had been granted
to the Neapolitans. The Pope then called to his
councils a man, Count Rossi, who had previously
been exiled from Rome, and had been branded
as a rebel. Count Rossi, however, when he was
about to take action to relieve the finances of
the country by means of a mortgage of Church
property, was assassinated as he was entering the
Capitol ; and upon his death the Cardinals proceeded to make arrangements with a view to re-
tracing the steps by which their authority had been
diminished. Their plans were discovered, but when
the people went in indignation to the Vatican and
implored the Pope to renew the oath to stand by
the constitutional form of government then existing,
and to disband his Swiss troops, he declined to
comply with their request, and eventually fled from
Rome in disguise.

Within a short time after the flight of the Pope
the Roman republic was established and the supreme
power vested in a triumvirate consisting of Mazzini,
Armellini, and Saffi. Clough, who arrived in Rome
shortly afterwards and paid a visit to Mazzini, states

that 'the temper of the people and the Assembly alike was clearly against the restoration of the temporal power,'—that he found Mazzini 'a less fanatical fixed-idea sort of man than he had expected,'—and that perfect tranquillity prevailed in the city. This Clough wrote in a letter to Mr. Palgrave in April, 1849, but, on the 16th of that month, M. Odillon Barrot announced in the National Assembly that the French Government had resolved on sending out an army to the Roman dominions with a view to the protection of their countrymen, the maintenance of legitimate French influence in Italy, and to obtain for the Roman population a good government. This army sailed the following week from Marseilles under General Oudinot, who, in addressing his troops, delivered the following remarkable observations,—

'The Government, resolved to maintain in all parts our ancient and legitimate influence, has been unwilling to leave the destinies of the people of Italy at the mercy of a foreign Power, or of a party forming only a minority. It confides to us the flag of France, in order that it may be planted on the Roman territory *as a marked testimony of our sympathy!*'

S

The expedition proceeded to Civita Vecchia, and
from thence the troops advanced on Rome, which
they besieged ; and after a bombardment lasting
about twenty days they succeeded in entering the
Eternal City, while the people screamed and hooted
'Viva la Reppublica Romana !' The free corps
under Garibaldi who had so bravely and heroically
defended Rome during the shameful siege retired
to the Abruzzi. And here, before returning to
Clough's poem, we would observe that it is by no
means clear what was the reason which led the
French Government to send this expedition to
Italy. They stated that their object was to pro-
mote the peace of the country and to establish a
constitutional government. The Earl of Aberdeen
on the contrary gave it as his opinion, in a speech
made by him shortly afterwards, that the expedition
was undertaken with a view more or less friendly to
the Papal Government, and to prevent action being
taken by the Austrians ;—while Lord Brougham,
speaking on the same evening, stated that he had
been present in Paris at the time, and that, from
what he had seen and heard, he did not believe
the French Government knew very distinctly, what
they meant in sending an army against another

republic, but that he thought the real reason was a desire to satisfy the craving of the mob for military glory. To this we will only add that M. Lesseps, who had been sent out as the plenipotentiary of France, signed a convention with the Roman Triumvirs before the siege commenced, by which military action would have been avoided, but General Oudinot refused to recognize this convention, and, declaring M. Lesseps' mission at an end, proceeded at once to make vigorous preparations for the instant prosecution of the siege. Thus the little Roman Republic under Mazzini and Garibaldi was destroyed ere it was many months old by the councillors of the Republic of France.

The *Amours de Voyage* contains Clough's views respecting this action on the part of France, very plainly stated in the following lines :—

' I, who avoided it all, am fated, it seems, to describe it.
I, who nor meddle nor make in politics,—I, who sincerely
Put not my trust in leagues nor any suffrage by ballot,
Never predicted Parisian millenniums, never beheld a
New Jerusalem coming down dressed like a bride out of
    heaven
Right on the Place de la Concorde,—I, nevertheless, let me
    say it,

Could, in my soul of souls, this day, with the Gaul at the gates, shed
One true tear for thee, thou poor little Roman Republic.
What, with the German restored, with Sicily safe to the Bourbon,
Not leave one poor corner for native Italian exertion ?
France, it is foully done !　and you, poor foolish England,
You, who a twelvemonth ago said nations must choose for themselves, you
Could not, of course, interfere ——'

And again—

'—— Meanwhile, notwithstanding all journals,
Honour for once to the tongue, and the pen of the eloquent writer !
Honour to speech ! and all honour to thee, thou noble Mazzini !'

These lines, although forming part of letters written by Claude, the hero of the *Amours de Voyage*, clearly set forth Clough's own opinions, for the views put forward are identical with those expressed in his own private correspondence, included in the first volume of the 'Poems and Prose Remains.' There are probably *now* very few persons in England who would be prepared to controvert his views on this subject, but such was not the case at the time when the facts were actually occurring :—It is, however, easy to be wise after the event.

The poem—it is really a novelette-in-verse—consists of a series of letters supposed to be written at Rome, in which is contained a full and interesting history of the love-adventures of the Englishman Claude, above referred to, who, while on a tour in Italy, makes the acquaintance of a family of the name of Trevellyn, and ultimately falls in love with one of the daughters. The letters are written by Claude, by Georgina, and by Mary Trevellyn respectively, and are enlivened by the different accounts given by the writers of their impressions of Rome, its scenes, its churches and Coliseum, its Forum and St. Peter's, its life and customs, &c. Miss Georgina writes, for instance, that 'Rome is a wonderful place,' but complains that it is 'not very gay.' Claude, on the other hand, declares that 'rubbishy' seems the word that most exactly would suit it, and that he is disappointed, save as regards the arch of Titus and the view from the Lateran : and he writes—

' Rome, believe me, my friend, is like its own Monte Testaceo,
Merely a marvellous mass of broken and castaway wine-pots.

*   *   *   *   *

" Brickwork I found thee, and marble I left thee ! " their Em-
     peror vaunted ;
" Marble I thought thee, and brickwork I find thee !" the
     tourist may answer.'

When someone suggested to Clough that this
poem was an account of his own (Clough's) doings
and experience during his visit to Italy, he very
emphatically replied that it was '*extremely* not so.'
This, we think, however, must have been intended
to apply mainly to the facts of the love-story, for
Claude clearly represents the poet in some other
respects, and the first letter in the poem, of which
Claude is the writer, puts forward the same views
and sentiments (in some sentences almost the same
words) as the reader will find put forward in a letter
written by Clough to his mother on the 18th April,
1849, from the Hôtel d'Angleterre, at Rome.   That
the character of Claude should bear a slight resemblance to that of the poet is only what one might
expect, but it is interesting to note how precisely
the following description of Claude, which we quote
from the ' Fortnightly Review,' of December, 1868,
pourtrays the characteristic features of Clough's
own idiosyncrasy : ' Claude is a young English
gentleman, well born and well connected, but na-

turally shy and rather satirical. His education has
rendered him fastidious, and he is by temperament
inclined to dream and meditate and question, rather
than to act. We soon find that he has the trick of
introspection and of nineteenth-century yearning
after the impossible.' Yet there is, after all, an
essential difference between the character of the
poet and that of the man whom he has depicted in
his poem, and we are driven to the conclusion that
Clough, being conscious of certain marked tendencies of his own temperament, his 'speculative
humour and subtle hesitancy of brain,' determined
to depict a man in whom these qualities, ironically
treated and somewhat intensified and exaggerated,
should serve as stumbling-blocks to any decisive
action whatever, and should, in the end, so prove
themselves their own *reductio ad absurdum.* This
hypothesis is in harmony with the poet's favourite
habit of critical introspection, and the irony which
he would at times direct against his own personal
characteristic qualities and his own natural tendencies of mind and body.

The sarcastic playfulness of the poet also appears
in the letters of Claude, and the following description which the latter gives of his new ac-

quaintances, the Trevellyns, is distinctly marked
with the sign and seal of the author :—

' Middle-class people these, bankers very likely, not wholly
Pure of the taint of the shop ; will at table d'hôte and
    restaurant
Have their shilling'sworth, their penny's pennyworth even :
Neither man's aristocracy this, nor God's, God knoweth !
Yet they are fairly descended, they give you to know, well
    connected ;
Doubtless, somewhere in some neighbourhood have, and are
    careful to keep, some
Threadbare genteel relations, who in their turn are enchanted
Grandly among county people to introduce at assemblies
To the unpennied cadets our cousins with excellent fortunes,
Neither man's aristocracy this, nor God's, God knoweth !'

These lines remind us of a sentence which occurs
in a letter from Clough to the late Dean Stanley,
written from Paris in May, 1848 : he writes—'It was
funny in the afternoon to see the classical virgins
walking about with their papas and mammas,
people of the under-shoe-making and back-street
shop-keeping class.'

Among the mottoes prefixed to the Amours de
Voyage is the line ' *Il doutait de tout, même de
l'amour,*' which very aptly illustrates and fore-
shadows the story of the poem, and is especially
applicable to the character of the hero.   The letters

of Claude beginning, as already intimated, with
accounts of Rome and reflections respecting its
history and religion, and continually referring to
the events of the siege, gradually pass into questions
of a more personal nature,—his acquaintance with
and feelings towards Mary Trevellyn, and into
metaphysical and interesting dissertations on the
nature and origin of Love. There are, he observes,
two kinds of human attraction,—the one disturbs
and unsettles, while the other poises, retains, fixes,
and holds you. But in his own case he fancies that
it is simply a matter of 'juxtaposition' as regards
Mary Trevellyn, and yet soon afterwards he
writes—

' But I have made the step, have quitted the ship of Ulysses ;
Quitted the sea and the shore, passed into the magical island ;
Yet on my lips is the *moly*, medicinal, offered of Hermes.
I have come into the precinct, the labyrinth closes around me,
Path into path rounding slyly ;—

    *   *   *   *   *

No, though she talk, it is music ; her fingers desert not the
     keys ; 'tis
Song, though you hear in the song the articulate vocables
     sounded,
Syllabled singly and sweetly the words of melodious meaning.
—I am in love, you say ; I do not think so, exactly.'

    *   *   *   *   *

From which we gather that, as is usual in these affairs of the heart, Claude was already in love, but did not know it, or, at any rate, was unwilling to admit it ;—and moreover, *il doutait de tout, même de l'amour.* Hence he allows day after day to depart, still remaining in a state of uncertainty both as regards his own feelings and those of the beloved one ; still waiting and watching, and trusting that love will prove 'its own inspiration and break into audible words.'

As Mary's sister Georgina writes about this time, 'he (Mr. Claude) is really too shilly-shally,'—and he himself appears to have been aware of his own deficiency in this respect, for he confesses,—

' Oh, 'tisn't manly, of course, 'tisn't manly, this method of wooing ;
'Tisn't the way very likely to win. For the woman, they tell you,
Ever prefers the audacious, the wilful, the vehement hero ;
She has no heart for the timid, the sensitive soul ; and for knowledge,—
Knowledge, O ye Gods !—when did they appreciate knowledge ?
Wherefore should they either ? I am sure I do not desire it.'

But while he is thus feebly wavering and hesitating, undecided as to what action he ought to

take, or what course to adopt, whether to advance
or retire,—while he is thus weakly temporizing,
great and important events are going on around
him, for the French army under General Oudinot
having advanced to Palo, to Monterone, and laid
up their guns at Santa Severa, had at last commenced the bombardment of Rome, and were now
in the midst of the fight. There is little need, we
presume, for us to call the reader's attention to the
irony which Clough has here so successfully employed in contrasting the stirring events of the
siege, the roar and thunder of battle, and the heroic
action of Mazzini and Garibaldi, with the doubts
and waverings, the indecision and perplexity, of a
hero who 'is really too shilly-shally!' Claude, on
entering the Caffè Nuovo, and ordering his usual
caffè-latte, is informed by the waiter—'*Non c' è
latte!*' And this is the sign that the battle has
begun ; and so he drinks his milkless *nero*, and
thinks of the Campidoglio Marbles. Afterwards
from the Pincian Hill, with Germans, Americans,
and others, standing in the sun, 'but afraid of a
probable shower,' he sees to the left of St. Peter's
the white smoke of the cannon and the black of
burning houses ;—he sees, too, the lines of men,

with gleaming bayonets, descending down the
vineyarded slopes.

Again on returning home from St. Peter's, having
crossed the bridge of St. Angelo and going towards
the Condotti, he encounters a crowd, and beholds
the swords smiting, then again upraised in the air
with blood trickling from them ;—stooping, he sees
'through the legs of the people the legs of a body,'
and on enquiry learns that it is a priest they have
killed, a priest who was attempting to fly to the
Neapolitan army.

In the meantime the Trevellyns, to escape from
those terrors of war, take their departure from
Rome, and start for Florence.   Claude was to have
accompanied them, but on the day before their
departure Georgina had instigated her *fiancè*, Mr.
Vernon, to speak to him 'about his intentions,
forsooth, and so forth.'   But being astounded and
horrified by this sudden proceeding, and just then
obtaining an offer of 'seeing the great Ludovisi
Collection,' he made that his excuse for remaining
at Rome, and wrote a letter explaining this alteration in his plans.   Thus the narrow little rivulet
of Separation is crossed and they are 'divided.'
The little stream widens and deepens, until at last

they perceive that it may be that they shall never meet again. Claude, of course, soon wishes to be once more with Mary Trevellyn. He wearies of St. Peter's, the solemn Rotonda, and the Vatican walls, and longs to be away—

'Where, upon Apennine slope, with the chestnut the oak-
    trees immingle,
Where, amid odorous copse bridle-paths wander and wind,'—

Adding—

'Ah, that I were far away from the crowd and the streets of
    the city,
Under the vine-trellis laid, my beloved, with thee !'

These elegiac lines remind us of those in Goethe's *Roman Elegies*—

'Eine Welt zwar bist du, O Rom ; doch ohne die Liebe
Wäre die Welt nicht die Welt, wäre denn Rom auch nicht
    Rom.' [1]

It is not improbable that it is to the *Roman Elegies* of Goethe we are indebted for the beautiful little elegiac poems that adorn the *Amours de Voyage*, as Clough was possibly led to adopt the

[1] 'Thou art indeed a world, O Rome ; and yet, were Love
    absent,
    Then would the world be no world, then would e'en
    Rome be no Rome.'

metre which his German master-poet had used in
writing during his residence amid the sacred buildings and ruins of Rome.   We do not know whether
Goethe was, like Clough, disappointed in a measure
with the Roman antiquities, but it is said that 'the
ever-pressing desire to discover the secret of vege-
table forms sent him meditative through the gardens
about Rome ; '—and his biographer, the late Mr.
Lewes, observes, 'Men who have never felt the
passion of discovery may rail at him (Goethe) for
thus, in Rome, forgetting, among plants, the quarrels
of the Senate and the eloquence of Cicero ; but all
who have been haunted by a great idea will sym-
pathise with him, and understand how insignificant
is the existence of a thousand Ciceros in comparison with a law of Nature.'

In Clough's little elegiac poems we notice, indeed,
a similar preference for the grandeur of Nature to
the wonders of Art and Antiquity ;—' the fair open
fields,' and ' Nemi, inurned in the hill,' are evidently
far dearer to him than the 'great Coliseum ' or the
Forum with its 'archway and two or three pillars.'
Something of this preference may, for instance, be
detected in the following graceful lines which are
inserted at the end of the Fourth Canto :—

' Therefore farewell, ye hills, and ye, ye envineyarded ruins !
　　Therefore farewell, ye walls, palaces, pillars, and domes !
Therefore farewell, far seen, ye peaks of the mythic Albano,
　　Seen from Montorio's height, Tibur and Æsula's hills !
Ah, could we once, ere we go, could we stand, while, to ocean
　　　　descending,
　　Sinks o'er the yellow dark plain slowly the yellow broad
　　　　sun,
Stand, from the forest emerging at sunset, at once in the
　　　　champaign,
　　Open, but studded with trees, chestnuts umbrageous and
　　　　old,
E'en in those fair open fields that incurve to thy beautiful
　　　　hollow,
　　Nemi, imbedded in wood, Nemi, inurned in the hill !—
Therefore farewell, ye plains, and ye hills, and the City
　　　　Eternal !
　　Therefore farewell !　We depart, but to behold you again !'

Where shall we find English elegiacs more
musical or more perfect than these !

But to return to Claude.—Weary of Rome, and
eager to be once more with Mary Trevellyn, he at
last determines to follow her to Florence ; but when
he reaches Florence he finds the Trevellyns have
gone on to Milan.　Shall he stay and look at the
pictures ? he asks himself ;—No, he is ' sick of the
statues and pictures,' and sets off at once by Bo-
logna and Parma to Milan.　But, unfortunately, on

arrival at Milan, he again found himself too late, for they had gone to Como. Then follows a fruitless chase, for by a sudden alteration in the plans of the Trevellyns, he loses them altogether, and travels in vain from place to place, through Bellaggio, over the Splügen, the Stelvio, etc., until at last he returns to Florence, and from Florence back again to Rome. In the end he relinquishes the pursuit in despair, and bows to the ruling of Providence and the Fates,—concluding the matter with the words :

'Faith, I think, does pass, and Love; but Knowledge
    abideth ;
Let us seek Knowledge ; the rest may come and go as it
    happens.'

Mary, meanwhile, was at Lucerne, half desponding, yet half hoping that he would still follow and find her. Too often, as she confesses in her last letter, had she looked for the little lake-steamer to bring him ; but now indeed she must no longer expect him. There is something extremely sad and piteous in the tone of these last words, and one feels that the tears are welling in the heart— the heart weary and love-bereaved.

Soon after this poem was published Clough, in

writing to his friend, Mr. C. E. Norton, observes—
'I have had, *mirabile dictu*, a letter from Emerson,
who reprimanded me strongly for the termination
of the *Amours de Voyage*, in which he may be
right and I may be wrong ; and all my defence can
only be, that I always meant it to be so, and began
it with the full intention of its ending so ; but very
likely I was wrong all the same.' Mr. Hutton,
however, does not think that he *was* wrong, for
he writes in his *Essays Theological and Literary*,
vol. ii. p. 247,—'Mr. Emerson has in some cases
shown himself a fine critic ; but he never made a
more egregious blunder than when he found fault
with Clough for not making this poem end more
satisfactorily. * * * * To my mind, the poem
would lose half its character and meaning if the
hero's incipiency of passion had been developed
into anything but incipiency ; if it had not faded
away just as it is represented as doing, with the
first difficulties, into a restless but still half-relieved
passiveness. The irony of the poem, with its background of Mazzinian and Garibaldian achievement,
would have been utterly spoiled by any other
conclusion.'

We must confess that when we first read the

T

Amours de Voyage we felt, like Mr. Emerson, that
the poem would have been more in accordance with
the tastes of the great majority of readers if it had
terminated more happily. Yet, on further consideration, no one will, we think, be prepared to controvert Mr. Hutton's wiser judgment in this matter.
To have made the poem end prettily would have
been in direct opposition to Clough's teaching
when he writes, ' Do we not work best by digging
deepest ? * * * by searching to display the
real thing ?' He did not manufacture mere pleasant fiction, but works so true to life, fact, and
reality—so perfectly harmonious throughout—so
truthful to Nature and the world in which we live—
that the reader unwittingly falls into the error of
supposing that he is reading history, and confi-
dently exclaims ' This is not fiction, this is no tale
by a romancer! it is the poet's own story—one of
the chapters out of his own autobiography.'

It has been observed that ' there is a singular
richness in the woof and textures of this poem, a
variety which we miss in compositions like *Werter*
or *Maud.*' There is, indeed, a wondrous mul-
tiplicity of allied forces brought together within
the compass of this original production, and per-

haps it would be difficult to find another poem equal to it in this respect. It is remarkable, moreover, for the testimony which it bears to the noble character of Mazzini, and the heroic defence of Rome :—it is also remarkable for the testimony of a very different kind which it supplies in respect of the Jesuits, as in the following lines :—

> ' Here you see them,—
> Here, with emasculate pupils and gimcrack churches of Gesu,
> Pseudo-learning and lies, confessional-boxes and postures,—
> Here, with metallic beliefs and regimental devotions,—
> Here, overcrusting with slime, perverting, defacing, debasing,
> Michael Angelo's dome, that had hung the Pantheon in heaven,
> Raphael's Joys and Graces, and thy clear stars, Galileo !'

In passing from the *Amours de Voyage* to the *Mari Magno, or Tales On Board*, we are, so to speak, taking a leap of a dozen years of the poet's life, as the former poem was composed in 1849 and the latter in 1861. To the events of those years it is intended to refer in a subsequent chapter. The first and perhaps the second of the 'Mari Magno' stories were written during a journey to Greece and Constantinople which he made for the

good of his health in the spring, the remainder
(with the exception of the last) were composed in
the following August while travelling in Auvergne
and the Pyrenees. They are for the most part
written in ten-syllable couplets—a metre very well
adapted, as has been pointed out, for the purposes
of story-telling in verse. It is, moreover, a metre
which is capable of being written in various modes
according to the taste and inclination of the poet ;
and the difference produced in its rhythm and
composition by the writers who have used it, is
very considerable. It has been observed that 'in
prose, the character of the vehicle for the composer's thoughts is not determined beforehand, but
that every composer has to make his own vehicle.'
And such is almost the case as regards this metre
of the ten-syllable couplet. It has been used by
numberless authors—by Chaucer, Dryden, Pope,
Goldsmith, Crabbe, and many others—but one has
only to compare the poetry of Chaucer with that of
Pope, to perceive that it has, when employed by a
new poet, often acquired an entirely different rhythm
and character. 'The Tales entitled *Mari Magno*
are in the plain, hard manner of Crabbe,' writes one
of Clough's reviewers ; and yet if the reader com-

pares the two following extracts, he will, we think,
agree that there is little similarity of manner, and
that even the metre is not quite the same :—

THE DYING SAILOR.

(By Crabbe.)

*　　*　　*　　*　　*

'He had his wish, had more ;　I will not paint
The lover's meeting : she beheld him faint,—
With tender fears, she took a nearer view,
Her terrors doubling as her hopes withdrew ;
He tried to smile, and, half-succeeding, said,
'Yes ! I must die ;' and Hope for ever fled.
　Still long she nursed him ; tender thoughts, meantime,
Were interchanged, and hopes and views sublime.
To her he came to die, and every day
She took some portion of the dread away :
With him she pray'd, to him his bible read,
Soothed the faint heart, and held the aching head.'

The following is from the second of the *Mari
Magno* tales :—

'Beside the wishing-gate which so they name,
'Mid northern hills to me this fancy came,
A wish I formed, my wish I thus expressed :
*Would I could wish my wishes all to rest,
And know to wish the wish that were the best !*
O for some winnowing wind, to the empty air

This chaff of easy sympathies to bear
Far off, and leave me of myself aware !
While thus this over-health deludes me still,
So willing that I know not what I will ;
O so for some friend, or more than friend, austere,
To make me know myself, and make me fear !
O for some touch, too noble to be kind,
To awake to life the mind within the mind !'

*   *   *   *   *

There is an ardent emotion, a fervent over-flowing of the soul, in these latter couplets, which we do not find in those by *Nature's sternest painter yet the best*, as Byron boldly designated Crabbe. Also, we notice an absence of the slow motion, the halting stiffness of the lines, which is so characteristic of the older poet. Yet in one respect there is indeed an undoubted similarity between the two bards, and the first portion of the following words which were written respecting Clough, are doubly applicable to Crabbe ;—'For his imagination at any time to abandon *terra firma* and console itself with cloudland would have been impossible. The fascination of the ideal was as strong for him as for other poets, but not stronger than the necessity of making it real.' One of the humorous authors of the *Rejected Addresses* has given to Crabbe the distinguishing title of *Pope in worsted stockings,*—yet we do not doubt that there are many amongst us at the present time who would hail with pleasure the advent of another poet who could depict human life with equal vigour and minuteness.

But it is to Chaucer, and not to Crabbe, that we must turn if we wish to find the prototype of these *Mari Magno* tales. Clough had been (as Mr. Palgrave tells us in his interesting Memoir), a careful student of Chaucer and our early English literature ; and in one of his Essays he (Clough) writes,—' In the age of Chaucer it may be said that the English people, such as ever since then it has been (and such never it had been till then) had, for good or for evil, or more truly for both, entered in various ways—in religion, in morals, in domestic habits, in government, in social relations, in relations to other members of the European body—upon a definite and positive course. * * * And the picture of all that pertains to those first exhibitions (for good or for evil, or for both) of our English genius and temper, you may see surviving unfaded in the lively colouring of the *Canterbury Tales ;* exhibitions, I have said, of genius and temper ; of dispositions, inclinations, tendencies, it is true, rather than of any formed and rigidly fixed determination. It is our boyhood ; but the man in looking back to it is conscious that that boyhood was his :—folded and compressed within the bud we detect the petals of the coming flower, the rudiment of the future fruit.'—It perhaps is not too much to state that in the *Canterbury Tales* we may, in a manner, behold the bud or boyhood of the *Mari Magno* tales. And in making this statement we are but following the suggestions of the writer, whose criticism of the poet is not only thoroughly appreciative, but is also the truest and best. He writes—' The oftener I return to Clough's unfinished but striking poems, the more I am struck by something in their fresh natural handling and a certain lustre of sunlight on their surface, which suggests to me a modern and intellectualised Chaucer; and I think the same homely breadth and simplicity were strongly marked in his countenance. * * * Had he lived to fill more completely with his individual genius, and to complete the beautiful fragments of tales which are entitled *In Mari Magno,* every one would have noticed not merely an external resemblance in structure and scheme, but a very close analogy in genius between the *Canterbury Tales* by the father of English poetry, and the series by this later representative of our academic school.'

This resemblance between the poetry of Chaucer and Clough's 'Mari Magno' stories has been referred to by others, as well as Mr. Hutton, from whose *Essays* the above is taken. An American author referring to these stories observes that we find in them 'a most concise directness, a truly Chaucerian simplicity.' But it is not solely as regards directness and simplicity that we find a similarity between the two poets ;—rather is it in the large and kindly view of life, which is common to both.

There is a 'perpetual fountain of good sense' sending up refreshing streams of truth and intelligence, in the writings of both poets. Each of them has, too, a characteristic power of graphically depicting, in a few words, various characters and persons, and we all remember Chaucer's 'Monk,' his 'Yeman,' and his 'Prioress,'

'That of hire smylyng was ful symple and coy '—

his 'Knight,' and his 'Squire,'—the latter

'Embroidered was he, as it were a mede

> Al ful of fresshe flowres, white and reede ;
> Syngynge he was, or floytynge,[1] al the day.'

There is something of the same pictorial power in Clough, and we actually behold, as we read, his ' Priest,' that

> ' Under his beaver sat and looked demure ;—
> Faintly he smiled the company to please,
> And folded held his hands above his knees.'

So also we seem to see the ' Postilion,'—he,

> 'in his smock of blue,
> His pipe into his mouth's far corner drew,
> And told about a farrier and a horse.'

While still more manifest is his ' English Clergyman '—

> 'spic and span
> In black and white—a large well-favoured man,
> Fifty years old, as near as one could guess,
> He looked the dignitary more or less.
> A rural dean, I said, he was, at least,
> Canon perhaps ; at many a good man's feast
> A guest had been, amongst the choicest there,
> Manly his voice and manly was his air.'

This, it should be observed, is the description given of the clergyman on board the vessel who is

---

[1] Fluting.

the narrator of two of the tales; but there is also another clergyman who is one of the principal characters in the first story, entitled *The Lawyer's First Tale;* and the close resemblance that is noticeable between these two would seem to imply that Clough painted their portraits from some clerical friend or acquaintance of his own, or possibly from some actual fellow-traveller on board with him during his passage to America.

The following are portions of the portrait of the second parson referred to in the *Lawyer's Tale:*—

> ' The vicar was of bulk and thewes,
> Six feet he stood within his shoes,
> And every inch of all a man ;
> Ecclesiast on the ancient plan,
> Unforced by any party rule
> His native character to school.
> In ancient learning not unread,
> But had few doctrines in his head ;
> Dissenters truly he abhorred
> They never had his gracious word.
> He ne'er was bitter or unkind,
> But positively spoke his mind.
> Their piety he could not bear,
> A sneaking, snivelling set they were.
>
> *　　*　　*　　*　　*
>
> Though sorry not to have a boy,
> His daughters were his perfect joy ;
> He plagued them, oft drew tears from each,

> Was bold and hasty in his speech ;
> All through the house you heard him call,
> He had his vocatives for all :
> Patty Patina, Pat became,
> Lydia took Languish with her name,
> Philippa was the Gentle Queen,
> And Phœbe, Madam Proserpine ;
> The pseudonyms for Mary Gwen
> Varied with every week again ;
> But Emily, of all the set,
> Emilia called, was most the pet.'

Of the six tales included in the *Mari Magno*, the second and the last are in some respects the most successful, though perhaps none of them are so powerful, none of them narrate so terrible a tale of human suffering and tears, as the fifth,—the clergyman's second tale.   Respecting it one is inclined to ask, ' Is it not too morbidly painful to be profitable ? Are we really any better for having passed through this joyless pilgrimage of sin and sorrow? Would not the time have been better spent,—more hopefully and more healthfully,—among the

> ' daffodils
> That come before the swallow dares, and take
> The winds of March with beauty ? '

There are two ways adopted by different persons of avoiding all that is wicked, horrible, and hurtful ;

the one is to be ever pondering on evil-doing and its
ill effects,—the other to put them from you, to turn
your attention to happier and nobler objects, and
thus to enjoy

' Sweet dreams, and health, and quiet breathing.'

Yet there will doubtless be persons who will be
pleased with this, the fifth of the *Mari Magno*
stories, as there are those whose delight it is to
witness the most tragic scenes of pain and suffering
represented on our London stage. Nay, indeed,
there are, in this our nineteenth century, thousands
of innocent souls of such culture and refinement,
that they can flock in enthusiastic crowds to behold
the hideous ravings of one rendered insane by
' drink ' ; or the scarcely less ghastly representation
in a play entitled ' The Bells,' by which so many were
enabled to sit and watch with pleasure the sicken-
ing spectacle of the changes passing over the
features of a dying man,—of a living human soul
apparently changing before their eyes into a livid
senseless corpse. But *chacun à son goût!*

In the second story, however, which is entitled
The Clergyman's First Tale, there is nothing very
painful,—nothing to greatly distress the mind of the

reader ; while the theory propounded towards the conclusion of the poem that *love is fellow-service*, is one not unworthy of the poet's teaching. Indeed, he has put forward the same, or nearly the same, view elsewhere, and in one of his letters he writes— 'the mere man's idea of a wife as a helpmate in duty is not in my judgment an insult to womankind, though it may require modification and correction. But if that were the worst sin committed against womankind, the world would be better than it is ; and many women, it appears to me, have been misled by their natural aversion to this into accepting worse things.'—This, if it be not a very ardent, or enthusiastic, view of love and marriage, is, at any rate, thoroughly sane and intelligent. *Love is fellow-service !* such is the moral of the story, which concludes with the unexpected meeting by the sea-shore of two old friends who had parted three years before without confessing their love :—

> ' Alone they met, from alien eyes away,
> The high shore hid them in a tiny bay.
> Alone was he, was she ; in sweet surprise
> They met, before they knew it, in their eyes.
> In his a wondering admiration glowed,
> In hers, a world of tenderness o'erflowed ;

>   *   *   *   *   *

The sea, perchance, and solitude had charms,
They met—I know not—in each other's arms.'

We quote these lines from the poem, as they appear to us to convey a deeper insight into the mystery of love than does the moral which Clough has appended to them. Let us say, then, if we will, ' Marriage ' is fellow-service, and is ordained of man,—the voluntary work of his own choice and intelligence. But love,—what is love ? It comes to us without our bidding, as it were some mighty impulse of the universe which encircles us, and of which we form a part :—it rises in our hearts, as the incoming tide of the ocean rises on the sea-shore, and we may not resist it :—it is a part of the might and magnetism of the mysterious forces of Nature, and we cannot fully explain it.

Chapter IX.

AMERICA RE-VISITED,

AND

PROSE WRITINGS.

WHEN Clough arrived in America,—whither,
as already stated, he had gone to try his
fortune, as a teacher and literary man,—his first step
was, as might be expected, to pay a visit to his old
friend, Ralph Waldo Emerson, at Concord. For
Emerson he appears to have always entertained
strong feelings of affection and admiration, and in
his letters written at this time he continually refers
to him in eulogistic terms, as being superior to the
other Americans whom he had met. Of Longfellow (who called upon him soon after his arrival),
he only observes that 'he is a very good fellow,'—
and had given him (Clough) an excellent English
dinner, including grouse, pheasants, and milk-

punch, at which Lowell and Norton were present. Emerson also had given a grand dinner-party in honour of 'the celebrated author of the *Bothie*' (as Clough was here designated), at which Hawthorne, Longfellow, Lowell, Theodore Parker, and Charles Sumner were amongst the guests. At this assembly we may say that the highest representatives of the genius and talent of America were present, and our English poet must have felt no little pleasure at so great a honour being paid to him so soon after his arrival in that country. His pleasure moreover would doubtless *not* be diminished when he remembered that a whole edition of the *Bothie of Tober-na-Vuolich* had previously been printed and sold in the United States, and had thus made his name known to the authors and other persons who were here invited to meet him.

Amongst the fair sex and the gay drawing-room circles of American society, he appears to have also met with a warm and appreciative reception, for in one of his letters he states—'A young lady, the other night, after I was introduced, told me she had had the pleasure of *looking* at me (the celebrated author !) at a party a few nights before. The force of compliment could no further go.'

U

The letters of Clough which are contained in the first volume of the *Poems and Prose Remains* are exceedingly pleasant reading, and few of them are more interesting than those written by him (apparently to his *fiancée*) about this time. The account given in them of the persons he met,—of the manners and customs of the people,—and of the scenery, climate, and character of the country, is both amusing and full of information. His powers of observation are nowhere more plainly indicated than they are in this correspondence, and after having perused some twenty pages of these printed extracts from his letters, one has almost as clear and intimate a knowledge of America and its people, as if one had oneself made a visit to Boston, U.S.

After he had made the acquaintance of so many illustrious members of American literary society, we are not surprised to find that Clough had no sooner settled down at his residence at Cambridge, Massachusetts, than he began to be furnished with pupils. In less than a week he was teaching Greek to his first Anglo-American student, a descendant of the old Governor Winthrop, of Cromwell's time : and shortly afterwards he writes that he is to de-

liver a lecture on English literature, from Chaucer
to Wordsworth. This appears to have been followed by two other lectures, one on the poet
Dryden, and the other on the poetry of Wordsworth ; while, in addition to these ' spoken essays,'
he wrote, during the eight months he was in
America, the *Two Letters of Parepidemus*, published in *Putnam's Monthly ;* a review of the poems
of Alexander Smith and Matthew Arnold, and one
of a work entitled *Considerations on some Recent
Social Theories,*—both of which appeared in the
North American Review, together with *A Passage
upon Oxford Studies*, extracted from a review of
the Oxford University Commissioners' Report,
1852. These, with the pamphlet on the Retrenchment Association at Oxford, and a review of Mr.
Francis Newman's book entitled *The Soul*, constitute the body of the prose writings of Clough, in
addition to the fragmentary *Notes on the Religious
Tradition.*

Of those who admire his poetry, there will, we
think, be found few that are not also pleased with
much that he has written in prose, although he (as
he himself was aware) has at times fallen into the
manner and method of Carlyle. It is to this fol-

lowing in the fashion of Carlyle that he refers when he writes,—'And now, O reader, farewell! Will you tell us that we are mere insignificant cetaceous flounderers sending up our puny spout after the pattern of that leviathan whom God has made to take his pastime therein? . . . . We have said, Look not up into the empty air, but upon the solid, somewhat dirty earth around, underfoot; and if we poor trumpeters do but bring the soldiers from the wrong ground to the right we shall be content, and shall trust that they, at least, will do something.'

It is, however, only occasionally that Clough has been tempted to depart from his own proper and natural style of prose composition, and to adopt that which we now all know so well as 'Carlylese.' The latter is, of course, more vehement and unrestrained, more fiery and dogmatic; but for calm, yet earnest, expression,—for plainly and convincingly stating the thought that he wished to convey to the reader, there are few styles preferable to that in which Clough usually wrote. As the subject of prose composition is attracting considerable attention at the present time, we will quote two extracts from Clough's writings,—the first being one in which he has most closely and plainly followed Carlyle,—the other a passage fairly representing his own style.

The first, the ' Carlylese,' is as follows :—

—' There is a religion whose revelation it is to be what religion so-called calls irreligion. It is, shall we say, Silence.

You have found out God, have you ? Why, who can it be that made all these contrivances for our comfortable existence here ; who put things together for us ; who built the house we live in, and the mill that we work in, and made the tools that we use ; who keeps the clock in order, and rings the bell for us, and lights the fire and cooks the victuals and lays the table for us ? Don't we find it laid every day ? Was it nobody, think you, that put salt in the sea for us ?

You have found out God, have you ? The vessel goes on its way : how ? You conclude there is someone, somewhere, working these wheels, these pistons, these strong and exquisitely-adapted means. Oh, my friends ! and, if in a dark room, under the main deck, you have hunted out a smudgy personage with a sub-intelligent look about the eyes, is that so great a gospel for me ? No ; not even should you go further, and signalise to me James Watt ! Am I, therefore, to fall down and worship ? No ; silly as it seems, if you insist upon my knee-dropping, I will worship rather the broad sea, the wavy hills, and the empty sky round about and above me, or the chance volume of I know not what in my hand. * * * * You have found out God, have you ? Ah, my friends ! let us be—*silent.*'

The above example of Clough's Carlylian prose is taken from his review of Mr. F. Newman's work, entitled *The Soul.* One cannot be greatly surprised that Clough should have imbibed some portion of Carlyle's characteristic manner, seeing that he was personally acquainted with him, and had experienced his strange power of conversation, of which Margaret Fuller Ossoli writes,—' He (Carlyle) pours upon you a kind of satirical, heroical, critical poem, with regular cadences, and generally catching up near the beginning some singular epithet which serves as a refrain when his song is full.'—Moreover, Clough had himself studied Carlyle's own master, so far as method is concerned, and in one of his letters he refers to Richter's proneness to 'sentiment,' adding, however, that in him it is not in its merely ' luscious form, but tempered with agreeable acids and delicate laurel-leaf bitters.'

But let us now give the other extract, or example of Clough's own ordinary style of composition :—

' The dream and aspiration,' he writes, ' of the ardent and generous spirits of our time is for a certain royal road to human happiness. Disappointed a thousand times, they still persist in their exalted creed that there must and will be here on earth, if not now, in some future and approaching time, a state of social arrangements in which the spontaneous action and free development of each individual constituent member will combine to form ' a vast and solemn harmony,' the ultimate perfect movement of collective humanity. There beautiful thoughts will distil as the dew, and fair actions spring

up as the green herb ; there, without constraint, we shall all
be good, and without trouble, happy ; there, what in its imperfect form is vice, shall gently and naturally flower out into
virtue ; there contention and contest, control and command-
ment, will be the obsolete terms of a dead language, with no
modern equivalents to explain them. A divine interior in-
stinct will intimate to each single human being his fittest
and highest vocation, and will prompt and inspire and guide
him to fulfil it ; while in the pursuit of his own free choice
and in the fulfilment of his own strongest desires, he will, by
the blessing of the presiding genius of humanity, best serve
the true interests of society and the race.

Was it not thus long ago ? For,

> Ante etiam sceptrum Dictæi regis, et ante
> Impia quam cæsis gens est epulata juvencis,
> Aureus hanc vitam in terris Saturnus agebat.

O blessed ages of pure, spontaneous, unconscious, unthinking,
unreasoning life and action, to you, either in the past or the
future, the human heart is still fain to recur—still must dream,
even though it be but a dream, of how sweet it were to grow
as the green herb, and bloom as the spring flowers, to be good
because we cannot be otherwise, and happy because we cannot
help it. O blessed ages, indeed ! But have such, since men
were men, ever been ? Or are such, while men are men, ever
likely to come ?'

In this paragraph,—which is taken from a review
of a work entitled *Considerations on some Recent
Social Theories,* published in the *North American
Review* for July, 1853,—there is nothing, we think,

to give offence; there is nothing gaudy or exaggerated; there is certainly no crotchety method, or mannerism; no fanciful *cachet* witnessing to the author; no tricks or devices of the artist. The thought of the writer is simply and plainly, yet eloquently expressed, and we feel that it would be difficult, if not impossible, to state the same truths as well and as forcibly in other language. Moreover, the sentences are not of that short and asthmatic description, which is so suggestive of the incompleteness produced by haste,—but the calm, well-balanced periods of one who writes at his leisure, and whose mind is accustomed to move in sustained flights through ample spaces. Lastly—and this is, perhaps, the most important point of all,—in this paragraph the writer does not in the too careful observance of the things that appertain to style, forget, or lose sight of, the fact that the manner must always be subservient to the subject-matter, and that a fine vehicle, however beautifully constructed, is practically of no use so long as there is nothing to carry in it. No one, probably, ever valued 'style' more highly, no one more thoroughly appreciated the necessity of perfect harmony between thought and word,—than did Clough, not-

withstanding that it has been said of him that he is
harsh and unadorned ; that he rough-hews like a
Cyclops, but cannot finish like a Canova. In his
paper on the poetry of Wordsworth he himself has
observed that 'some of the highest truths are only
expressible to us by style, only appreciable as indicated by manner.' Yet no one will ever charge
Clough with being either over-careful as regards his
language being polished and euphonious, or with
being not sufficiently careful as regards the importance of the truths that he wished to convey to the
reader. With him there is 'no wilful waste of language verging on a woful want of sense.'

In his two *Letters of Parepidemus* the theory is
propounded that as we advance, as the human race
moves onward, and possibly upward, the whole perspective changes around us, and whether we will or
not, we behold the landscape in an entirely different
light to that in which preceding ages beheld it. We
are like travellers passing through changeful scenery,
and they who know the country may show us at
each new stage the high mountain summits we are
retiring from ; may 'point out the Mont Blanc
whose shadow we stood in at Chamouni, in its full
magnificent outline at Sallanches, and again, far

distant, yet not less rose-tinged, at sunset from
Geneva.' . . . . The high peaks of past religions,
the magnificent outlines of ancient mythologies,
the receding forms of more modern beliefs, the
rose-tinged, or shall we say, the sanguine-tinted
dogmas and doctrines disappearing in the peaceful
twilight—all, all of them are changed, and still
changing, both as regards position and appearance,
in the human perspective. 'Twenty-five years
have I spent in learning,' said the young man to the
old. 'Return,' said the sage, 'and spend another
twenty-five in unlearning.'—'Each new age,' writes
Clough, ' and each new year has its new direction ;
and we go to the well-informed of the season before
ours, to be put by them in the direction which, because right for their time, is therefore not quite
right for ours.'

But, we would ask, is this so ? Is it true that
what was right for the preceding age is therefore
not quite right for our own ? How eager no doubt
will some of our conservative readers be to reply,
'Certainly not! What was right yesterday, is right
to-day, and will be right *in sæcula sæculorum.*' Yet
again we would ask, is it so ? Do not our environments change, and must not each organism alter its

conduct and course of action in order to adapt itself
to the altered condition of affairs in which it must
necessarily live ? As the seasons of the year succeed
each other we alter our apparel to meet the require-
ments of summer heat, or winter's snow ;—and in
each succeeding age the circumstances and conditions of life will be found to have changed, to have
grown and developed, into something different
from what they were before.   Are we to wear our
overcoats during the tropical heat of the dog-days !
There was a time, for instance, when education, and
erudition, and even the ability to read, or to write,
were confined to the Catholic priests, and a few,
a very few, others.   In those days it was right no
doubt that those who were ignorant, and were
unable to read or study for themselves, should be
guided by Authority, and should abide by the
teaching of those who had read in the great volumes
of the writers of antiquity, and who were so far in
advance of themselves.   It was right, we repeat, in
those days of darkness that men in their ignorance
should not so much believe in their own individual
judgment, as in the infallibility of their Church and
their religious instructors, and in the great Catholic
maxim, *Quod semper, quod ubique, quod ab omnibus.*

But if the time has now arrived when the higher
and middle classes, and even a portion of the poorer
classes, are sufficiently educated to form a correct
judgment on most subjects, and if further, so far as
science and philosophy are concerned, many of them
are in advance of their religious teachers, then it is
no longer right that they should accept the infallibility of Authority, or even the creed of their own
sect or country, instead of thinking and judging
for themselves.   Rather should they take as their
example the child Lamennais, who when only eight
years of age, gazing upon a stormy waste of waters,
thought he beheld the Infinite, and said to himself
of those beside him,—' They are looking at what I
am looking, but they do not see what I see !'   We
do not mean by this that it is right to over-estimate
our own judgment, or to think that we know better
than every-body else; but only that each person after
listening to the advocates on both sides, and after
' getting to know on all matters which most concern
him the best which has been thought and said in
the world,' should then himself give the casting
vote,—should then at last decide and judge for
himself.

To return, however, to Clough, it has always

appeared to us to be a matter for regret that he did not leave behind him a larger amount of prose writing. It is stated as regards his poetry that he composed slowly and with difficulty, yet it must not be forgotten that his poems cover five-hundred pages, and are therefore in bulk almost equal to the original poems by Gray, Goldsmith, and Coleridge, added together. His prose essays, on the other hand, only fill about half that number of pages. With reference to this scantiness of production, Mrs. Clough in the memoir prefixed to the ' Poems and Prose Remains ' observes,—' His brain though powerful was slow to concentrate itself, and could not carry on several occupations at once. Solitude and repose were necessary for production. This, combined with a certain inertia, a certain slowness of movement, constantly made it hard for him to get over the initial difficulties of self-expression, and would often, no doubt, cause him to delay too long and lose the passing inspiration or opportunity. But, once started, his very weight carried him on, as it did in the *Bothie,* the *Amours de Voyage, Dipsychus,* and *Mari Magno.*' During his visit to America Clough appears to have for a time thrown off this inertia, and to have moved forward with no little alertness and determination. Indeed, the amount of work which he succeeded in completing in the brief period of nine months is somewhat surprising, for in addition to lectures, teaching, and visiting, he wrote some six ' essays,' and completed a considerable portion of the revision of the translation, known as Dryden's, of Plutarch's *Lives,* which he had undertaken for an American publisher. Nor was he by any means free from interruption, for in one of his letters he writes,—' Only ten pages of Plutarch done to-day. But at twelve Emerson appeared, and after sitting awhile with me, took me off to dine in town with him.' This, and some other portions of his letters, remind one somewhat of the entries in *Pepys' Diary,* as for instance when he (Clough) writes, —' Just come back from a little party, to which I went in a very bad humour, but have returned in much better!' On the other hand, quite a little ' golden treasury ' of good things might easily be collected together from the various passages of wit and wisdom which are to be found in Clough's letters. Humorous anecdotes, sunny descriptive pictures of the country, and shrewd precepts from the philosophy of common-sense, are mingled together after the manner of a perfect piece of literary patch-

work. Here, for instance, are four examples which
we find not far apart, and which will serve to indicate
to the reader the richness of the soil from which these
flowers are taken :—

‘ Did I tell you of the aged Calvinist woman, who, being
asked about the Universalists, said, “ Yes, they expect that
everybody will be saved, but ‘ we look for better things ’”?’

‘ On Sunday I walked across a bit of wood and got into a
bog, which was all covered with the blue Iris. I picked also
some Andromeda and Kalmia.’

‘ Energy is a very ordinary thing ; reasonableness is much
less common, and does ten times the good.’

‘ Emerson’s little girl brought in some small “ pensées,”
which she called “ lady’s delights,” and some other little
things that did for flowers. Edith is a very nice child, and
will be eleven next Monday. “ When I was going to be nine
years old, I didn’t know how I should feel.” “ Well, and
how did you feel ? ” “ Oh, I didn’t feel anyhow.”’

In reading over these letters written by Clough
in America, we notice the first signs of failing
health in the numerous complaints which he makes
respecting the changeableness of the weather, and
the cold, damp climate, which manifestly did not
suit him. Again and again he refers to the subject,
occasionally adding that the change in the tempe-
rature had given him a rheumatic cold or a sore
throat,—those little hints, or intimations of Nature,

which tell us that things are not quite as they ought to be. However, he was fortunately not destined to remain much longer in such close proximity to the region of the icebergs, for as a letter from Emerson in the preceding August had summoned him to America, so now a letter from Carlyle called him back again to England, where his friends had obtained for him an examinership in the Education Department. In June, 1853, he bid farewell to his American companions, who had by this time become rather numerous, and embarking on board the good ship "Asia," sailed once more for his native country.

Chapter X.

LAST YEARS.

AMONG the various lyric poems which Clough has left us, there is a little group, fourteen in number, clustering together under the title of *Songs in Absence*. These were composed, some of them during his outward and homeward passages across the Atlantic, and some whilst he was residing at Cambridge, U.S. They are in many respects typical of his method of composition, and especially of his practice of producing certain pleasing effects by the repetition of words, sounds, and phrases,—returning again and again to the same verse, word, or thought, as though it was so true or so beautiful, that his muse would still fain hover around it. In one it is the hope of meeting again upon some future day,—

> ' Some future day when what is now is not,
> When all old faults and follies are forgot,

And thoughts of difference passed like dreams away,
We'll meet again, upon some future day.

     *　　　*　　　*　　　*　　　*

Some day, which oft our hearts shall yearn to see,
In some far year, though distant yet to be,
Shall we indeed,—ye winds and waters, say !—
Meet yet again, upon some future day ?'

In another it is the cry, *Come home, come home!*

     *　　　*　　　*　　　*　　　*

' Come home, come home ! and where a home hath he
Whose ship is driving o'er the driving sea?
Through clouds that mutter, and o'er waves that roar,
Say, shall we find, or shall we not, a shore
That is, as is not ship or ocean foam,
              Indeed our home ?'

These love-songs, addressed by the poet to the lady who afterwards became his wife, have one especial characteristic, namely, the difference in tone and expression which distinguishes them from ordinary modern erotic verse. In the place of passionate outbursts, or simple love-sick lyrics, we have this cluster of poems written in the 'region of a clearer air,' and chanted by spirit unto spirit, in the 'dwelling of a purer love.' They are, so far as we are aware, the only verse that Clough composed during his visit to America, with the exception of the poem on the *Last Words of Napoleon and Wellington*, which was published in *Fraser's Magazine*.

Within a month from the date of Clough's return to England he commenced work at the Education Department as an examiner,—as he states in a letter to Mr. C. E. Norton, '*operose nihil agendo*—very *operose*, and very *nihil* too!' This, it need hardly be observed, was written nearly thirty years ago, and long before the commencement of our modern Educational reform ; doubtless our friends who are examiners at the present time would tell a very different story, and would say, '*operose*, perhaps, but by no means *nihil !* ' However, it is interesting to note that even in those far-off days the approaching change had apparently begun to loom in the distance, for the poet in another letter to Mr. Norton, writes,—' Bright, you see, has for the first time come out for the secular system. * * * * And certainly all through the land the secular schools should receive government subsidies, from which at present they are excluded.'

But in addition to his official labours, (which he probably found increased as he became more conversant with the work,) Clough at this time continued the revision of the translation of Plutarch which he had begun in America. This was in due course perfected and published, and must not be overlooked as forming an important addition to the work which he completed during the brief thirteen years that remained to him after leaving Oxford. In June, 1854, he married, and his marriage would seem to have rendered the latter portion of his life happier, and more hopeful and contented, than the solitary days of his bachelorhood could possibly have been.

Two years later, as we are told in the memoir prefixed to 'The Poems and Prose Remains,' p. 46, ' he was appointed Secretary to a commission for examining the scientific military schools on the continent. He visited in consequence the great schools for artillery and engineers in France, Prussia, and Austria. The travelling lasted about three months, and besides being very interesting and agreeable, it afforded him much occupation during a considerable time afterwards. Another employment, which frequently fell to him, was the examining of candidates in his own special subject of English literature, sometimes for Woolwich, sometimes in his own office. But the work in which

he took the deepest interest was that of his friend
and relation, Miss Florence Nightingale. He
watched over every step in her various under-
takings, affording her assistance not merely with
advice, and little in his life gave him greater satisfaction than to be her active and trusted friend.'—
This lady, Miss Nightingale, was, we may mention,
his wife's first cousin, and in one of his letters to
Mr. Norton we notice that he writes, ' I went over to
Calais last Saturday night, to see Florence Nightingale so far on her way to Scutari. She has ten
Sisters of Mercy proper, eight of Miss Sellon's, six
of a sort of Via Media institution, and ten other
nurses under her charge.' Another of his letters
to Mr. Norton, dated June, 1854, is written from
Lea Hurst, Matlock, Miss Nightingale's charming
and romantic residence, which we remember to
have visited while staying at Matlock in the year
1858.

During the first six years after his return from
America Clough does not appear to have been very
productive as a poet. Indeed, this period, and that
of his undergraduate life at Oxford, may be described as almost barren as regards poetry. There
are, however, some pleasant lines *To a Sleeping*

Child probably composed about this time, and there are several other poems the date of the composition of which appears to be uncertain. As some of these are far too important to be passed over, we will take this opportunity of referring to those which especially claim our notice, and of which we have not hitherto spoken. Amongst them are several compositions of a fragmentary description, as for instance the *Mystery of the Fall.* This poem, in our judgment, does great injustice to Clough, and we do not think that he would himself have published many portions of it as they at present stand. The lines beginning the second scene are quite unworthy of the poet, and have already furnished one unkind reviewer with an unfavourable example of Clough's poetry. It is very hard on an author when an unfinished and imperfect composition, found after his death amongst the old papers in his study, is not only printed and published, but is afterwards put forward by a reviewer as a representative specimen of his work and severely criticised—yet this is what has occurred in the case of Clough's *Mystery of the Fall.* It only remains to state that the title has been added since the poet's death, the fragment having been found in a very imperfect condition, and without any title appearing on the MS.

But there is another incomplete poem, *The Shadow*, of which we would speak in very different terms. It contains, in little more than one hundred lines, all the qualities which are especially characteristic of Clough's poetry. In it we have the clear-aired, graphic description, of which he was so skilful a master, accompanied by the most tender and touching pathos, and the most subtle, penetrating irony. It is too long for us to quote it *in extenso*, and to give extracts would be to do it an injustice. We are glad, however, to notice that Mr. T. H. Ward has included it amongst the examples of Clough's work given in his *English Poets*, vol. iv. To those, who on reading this poem of *The Shadow*, feel somewhat despondent, and apprehend a future in which irreligion shall reign triumphant, we would repeat the following words of Professor Goldwin Smith,—'The philosophy of history,' he writes, 'in its highest sense, as was before said, is the offspring of a great truth which has but recently dawned upon mankind. That truth is the moral unity of the human race; the softening down of mere dogmatic and ecclesiastical divisions between different parts of Christendom, the intercourse, the moral relation, the treaties and the bonds ratified by common appeals to God, into which Christendom has entered with nations beyond its pale, have let in the conviction that Virtue and Truth, however they may vary in their measure, are in their essence the same everywhere, and everywhere divine. * * * If the churches of Hildebrand, Luther, and Calvin, are passing away, above them rises that church of *pure religion and virtue* to which in their controversies with each other they have all implicitly appealed, and which therefore is above them all. A certain man was hung by his enemies blindfold over what he supposed to be a precipice with a rope in his hands ; he clung till his sinews cracked, and he had tasted the bitterness of death ; then, letting go the rope, he found that he had been hanging but half-a-foot from the ground.'

Of Clough's other poems, which we have not yet referred to, we may mention *The Latest Decalogue*, a witty satire of ' worldly holiness,'—and *Ite Domum Saturæ, venit Hesperus*. The latter is the rhymed monologue of a peasant girl driving her cows (Rose, Provence, and La Palie) homewards at eventide,— possibly the same peasant beauty as the one of the

Pyrenees, referred to in the *Mari Magno* tales, 'who fed her cows the mountain peaks between.' In this poem she is lamenting the absence of her lover, and wondering whether in his slumbering he sometimes sees the 'feeding kine,' and whether he thinks of her. 'For,' she sings,—

> ' Weary is work, and weary day by day
> To have your comfort miles on miles away.
> (Home, Rose, and home, Provence and La Palie.)'

Adding,—

> ' Or may it be that I shall find my mate,
> And he returning see himself too late ?
> For work we must, and what we see, we see,
> And God he knows, and what must be, must be,
> When sweethearts wander far away from me.
> (Home, Rose, and home, Provence and La Palie.)'

*　　*　　*　　*　　*

The majority of poets would have painted their peasant-girl as a model of faithfulness to her absent lover,—not so Clough ; he painted human nature precisely as he found it, and if critics or strangers objected, we doubt not that he replied,

> ' He could not know,
> But it was truth, the fact was so.'

There is, however, no doubt that the series of

poems which are brought together under the title of *Religious Poems,* are the finest of Clough's lyrical compositions. The lines *Through a Glass Darkly,* and *Perchè pensa? Pensando s' invecchia* are excellent,—as also are those beginning, *O Thou whose image in the shrine.*—But in parting with the poet's verse we will venture to quote a poem not included in this series; it is one with which many readers will be already conversant, and which should not be omitted from this volume.

'THE STREAM OF LIFE.

' O stream descending to the sea,
　　Thy mossy banks between,
The flow'rets blow, the grasses grow,
　　The leafy trees are green.

' In garden plots the children play,
　　The fields the labourers till,
And houses stand on either hand,
　　And thou descendest still.

' O life descending into death,
　　Our waking eyes behold,
Parent and friend thy lapse attend,
　　Companions young and old.

' Strong purposes our mind possess,
　　Our hearts affections fill,

We toil and earn, we seek and learn,
  And thou descendest still.

' O end to which our currents tend,
    Inevitable sea,
To which we flow, what do we know,
    What shall we guess of thee ?

'A roar we hear upon thy shore,
    As we our course fulfil ;
Scarce we divine a sun will shine
    And be above us still.'

The date of these lines is not given, but we may safely assume that they were composed during the last decade of the poet's life.

In the meantime those last years were slipping away, happily and pleasantly, and were bearing him down to the 'inevitable sea' of which he writes so thoughtfully in the lines we have just quoted. Occasionally, we are told, he employed his leisure moments in revising the *Bothie*, which he considerably improved, as the reader may easily discover for himself by comparing the first edition of 1848 with the poem as it is now published. He also occasionally returned to his favourite employment of translating Homer, and some of his translations from the Iliad will be found amongst the *Essays in*

Classical Metres included with his original poems.
In September, 1859, he removed from his residence
near the Regent's Park, and went to live at 21,
Campden Hill Road, Kensington, close to the
house in which Lord Macaulay at that time resided.
It is to be regretted that this change of residence
took place, seeing that almost immediately afterwards Clough was laid up with an attack of
scarlatina, and from the date of that illness his
health appears to have gradually broken down.
The following is the account of the last years of his
life given by Mr. William Allingham in a paper
published in 1866 :—

'Clough's health, at no time very strong, after
1859 began to give cause for anxiety. He had an
illness in the winter, not serious but weakening,
and in the summer of 1860 a slight accident to his
foot had a depressing effect. In November, getting
leave of absence from the Education Office, he went
to Malvern, and in February, 1861, to Freshwater,
Isle of Wight, where he improved, and spent some
happy weeks with his wife and children, and in the
middle of April started upon a short tour to Greece
and Constantinople. In June he returned to England, seeming to long for home ; he was languid

and depressed, and spoke little of his journey. In
July he went to the Pyrenees, in September joined
his wife in Paris, whence they travelled south, by
the Simplon to Lago Maggiore. 'The sense of
southern beauty and richness seemed to penetrate
him with enjoyment.' They 'made expeditions to
Isola Bella, Orta, and Magadino; but here he
became slightly unwell and hurried on to Milan.'
Here he was able to go about a little, 'but never
recovered himself; and they continued their painful
journey, during which he grew gradually worse, to
Florence, where they expected to meet friends, and
where they found good medical help. Some days
were better than others, and at Parma he spent a
few hours among the pictures of Correggio with
great enjoyment. The last day before entering
Florence they had a drive of several hours over the
Apennines, coming down over Pistoia. It was a
lovely sunny day; the hills were covered with
young chestnuts and flowering arbutus; the air was
fresh and soothing, and he seemed to revive on the
heights, but looked with dread on the sultry plain
lying beneath, with its white towns shining hot in
the sun. They reached Florence early in the day
of October 10th. That afternoon Arthur went to

the Boboli gardens, and to look at the grand arches
of Orcagna in the Piazza del Granduca. The next
day, too, he attempted to walk as far as the Cathe-
dral and the Baptistery, which were close to the
hotel; but on the 12th, when a permanent lodging
had been found, he went to bed, unable any longer
to resist the fever.'

'The fever, a sort of malaria, had its course and
appeared to give way. During the first three weeks
he seemed perpetually occupied with a poem he
was writing, the last in the volume of his poems
(one of the *Mari Magno* tales), and when he began
apparently to recover, and was able to sit up for
several hours in the day, he insisted on trying to
write it out, and when this proved too great an
effort he begged to dictate it. But he broke down
before it was finished, and returned to bed never to
leave it again.' This poem, or a form of it,
was found written in pencil in one of his note-
books. 'The fever left him worn out, and then
paralysis, with which he had been threatened,
struck him down. On the 13th of November he
died, in his forty-third year. His body was laid in
the little Protestant cemetery outside the walls of
Florence, looking towards Fiesole.'

In the same sacred resting-place lie also the bodies of two other illustrious and much beloved poets, Walter Savage Landor, and Elizabeth Barrett Browning:—'tall cypresses,' we are told, 'wave over the graves, and the beautiful hills keep guard around.'

Chapter XI.

CONCLUSION.

'HOW can I help remembering what a mind and character we have lost in losing Mr. Clough, whose name has more than once occurred in my lectures on Homer? He, too, was busy with Homer; but it is not on that account that I now speak of him. Nor do I speak of him in order to call attention to his qualities and powers in general, admirable as these were. I mention him because, in so eminent a degree, he possessed these two invaluable literary qualities: a true sense for his object of study, and a single-hearted care for it. He had both; but he had the second even more eminently than the first. He greatly developed the first through means of the second. In the study of art, poetry, or philosophy, he had the most undivided and disinterested love for his object in itself, the greatest aversion to mixing up with it anything accidental or personal. His interest was in literature itself; and it was this which gave so rare a stamp to his character, which kept him so free from all taint of littleness. In the saturnalia of ignoble personal passions, of which the struggle for literary success, in old and crowded communities, offers so sad a spectacle, he never mingled. He had not yet traduced his friends, nor flattered his enemies, nor disparaged what he admired, nor praised what he despised. Those who knew him well had the conviction that, even with time, these literary arts would never be his. His poem, ' *The Bothie of Toper-na-Fuosich,*' has some admirable Homeric qualities; out-of-doors freshness, life, naturalness, buoyant rapidity. Some of the expressions in that poem,—' *Dangerous Corrievreckan* ' . . . . ' *Where roads are unknown to Loch Nevish,*' —come back now to my ear with the true Homeric ring. But that in him of which I think oftenest is the Homeric simplicity of his literary life.'

Such is the testimony which Mr. Arnold in his *Last Words on Translating Homer* so ably contributes to the memory of his friend,—to his single-heartedness, to his nobility of mind and character. Such testimony leaves little to be desired, and little

Y

can any poor words of ours add to its value or completeness. Yet in stating that Clough's 'interest was in literature itself,' one would fain observe that this interest in literature was subordinate to the higher, holier interest which he took in the pursuit of truth, and more especially of religious truth. Towards science and the facts which scientific research is slowly but surely adding to the storehouse of human knowledge, he had not so strong, so enthusiastic an inclination. Indeed, it might almost be said that the development of his intellectual nature in this respect was somewhat defective, were it not that the tendency of his mind to seek above all things accuracy and exactness, is especially in unison with the teaching of modern science.

This tendency in Clough was, however, chiefly exhibited, first, in endeavouring to solve the complex problems of the universe, and secondly, in his attempt to find a firm and satisfactory basis for that higher spirituality which shall, in practical everyday life, blossom into noble action. As regards the first of these, it may be that Clough completely failed in his endeavours, but who, after all, is prepared to say that he did ?—It may be that, like Goethe, his position was on the border-lands that

lie between dogma and denial, and that the lines
which Faust addresses to Margaret most adequately
express his views, the lines—

> ' Him who dare name?
> Or who proclaim,
> Him I believe?
> Who feel,
> Yet steel
> Himself to say ; Him I do not believe.'

But, after all, it does not indeed very much matter
whether Clough succeeded or not, so long as he
was possessed of what is far more precious than
truth itself, namely, the love of truth, and the
earnest desire to seek after, and if possible, to
obtain it.

It is this desire,—this eager seeking after Truth,
that constitutes the main resemblance between
Clough and the Roman poet Lucretius. 'These
two men,' observes an able writer in the *Quar-
terly Review* for April, 1869, 'were philosophers
not from the desire of fame, not from the pleasure of intellectual discovery, not because they
hoped that philosophy would suggest thoughts
that would soothe some private grief of their
own, but because it was to them an overpowering

interest to have some key to the universe, because all even of their desires were suspected by them until they could find some central desire on which to link the rest; and love and beauty, and the animation of life, were no pleasure to them, except as testifying to that *something beyond* of which they were in search.' There is, however, no necessity to press too closely the analogy that may exist between the compositions of these two poets, and indeed, beyond that referred to in the above quotation, the similarity between them is not very striking. But, in addition to the fact that the minds of both poets loved to dwell on the highest subjects, and would fain press forward into the region of the Unknown, there is one other point of resemblance that must not be overlooked, and that is their *sincerity*. They were not simply artists in the arrangement of harmonious words, but the unveilers of their own hearts and minds, the revealers of a religion which, if not new, was nevertheless very precious to them as containing what in their inmost souls they believed to be the truth. Their poetry took for its subject that which they revered and loved, while they strove to embalm the truths of their own religion in the beauty and melody of

verse. Other poets have done the same,—have had
vital thoughts and over-mastering convictions
within them,—have had a real, living, and energy-
giving religion of their own, and have not been
afraid to preach and teach it in their verse. It will
suffice to mention one, and that one shall be Burns,
—a bard, in many respects, very different from him
of whom we write, and yet how extremely apposite
to both are the following words, written by Thomas
Carlyle, respecting the Ayrshire peasant, the
greatest of Scottish poets :—

'The excellence of Burns is, indeed, amongst the
rarest, whether in poetry or prose ; but, at the same
time, it is plain and easily recognized : his Sincerity,
his indisputable air of Truth. Here are no fabulous
woes or joys; no hollow fantastic sentimentalities ;
no wire-drawn refinings, either in thought or
feeling : the passion that is traced before us has
glowed in a living heart ; the opinion he utters has
risen in his own understanding, and been a light to
his own steps. He does not write from hearsay,
but from sight and experience; it is the scenes that
he has lived and laboured amidst, that he describes ;
those scenes, rude and humble as they are, have
kindled beautiful emotions in his soul, noble

thoughts, and definite resolves; and he speaks
forth what is in him, not from any outward call of
vanity or interest, but because his heart is too full
to be silent. He speaks it with such melody
and modulation as he can; 'in homely rustic
jingle;' but it is his own, and genuine. This is the
grand secret for finding readers and retaining
them: let him who would move and convince
others, be first moved and convinced himself.
Horace's rule, *Si vis me flere*, is applicable in a
wider sense than the literal one. To every poet, to
every writer, we might say: Be true, if you would
be believed. Let a man but speak forth with
genuine earnestness the thought, the emotion, the
actual condition of his own heart; and other men,
so strangely are we all knit together, by the tie of
sympathy, must and will give heed to him. In
culture, in extent of view, we may stand above the
speaker, or below him; but in either case, his
words, if they are earnest and sincere, will find some
response within us; for in spite of all casual
varieties in outward rank, or inward, as face answers
to face, so does the heart of man to man.'

And this is not only true of poetry, but it is true
also of all literary work; nor, indeed, is it confined to

literature,—it is equally applicable to the ordinary conduct of life and to our daily intercourse with our fellow men ; to the life of Action as well as to the life of Thought.

For the majority of mankind action, and not thought, is the characteristic function of our human existence, while the daily labour and the earning of 'daily bread,' leave the busy worker but little leisure for pondering over, or considering, abstract subjects that do not concern his immediate welfare. To the poet, to the man of letters, the philosopher or the artist, the reverse of this is more or less the natural condition of life, and thought to a very considerable extent supplants and takes the place of action. The life of Clough was, for the most part, of this latter description, yet the Sincerity, which Carlyle so highly appraises, is not only apparent in Clough's thought and poetry, but is also conspicuous in the conduct and practice of his daily life. The fact that he did not hesitate to relinquish his Fellowship at Oxford, as soon as he felt that he could not conscientiously hold it, is alone sufficient to indicate what manner of man he was. There is, however, another incident in the poet's life to which the *Athæneum*, in reviewing

'The Poems and Prose Remains,' called attention many years ago as illustrating, in a remarkable manner, the Christian kindliness of Clough's nature. The story has since been repeated by more than one writer, but the following is the brief statement of the facts contributed by Professor Shairp to Mrs. Clough's memoir prefixed to the poet's works :—'He (Clough) also visited the house by the side of Loch Ericht, a small heather-thatched hut, occupied by one of the foresters of the Ben Aulder forest. He found one of the children lying sick of a fever, the father I think from home, and the mother without any medicines or other aid for her child. He immediately set off and walked to Fort William, about two days' journey from the place, but the nearest place where medicines and other supplies were to be had. These he got at Fort William, and returned on his two days' journey, and left them with the mother. He had four days' walk over a rough country, to bring medicines to this little child, and the people did not even know his name. On these occasions in Scotland, he told me that he used to tell the people he was a 'Teacher,' and they were at once at ease with him then. I doubt whether he ever mentioned this to anyone but myself, and to me it only came out casually.'

The kindliness of this charitable action will be most fully appreciated by those who have a lively recollection of the roughness of the country lying round and about Loch Ericht. One who visited both Loch Ericht and Fort William only two months ago, states that a more wild, wet, roadless country, than that which intervenes between these two places he does not remember to have ever met with.

In a preceding chapter of this volume a paragraph which occurs in one of Clough's letters was referred to, in which he had urged that 'it is a good deal forgotten that we came into this world to do not kindness to others, but our own duty, to live soberly, righteously, and godly, not benevolently, philanthropically, and tender-heartedly:'—and it was pointed out that the reverse of this might be taught with equal force and with greater advantage to the world at large. This incident just narrated, this act of benevolence and tender-heartedness done to the little child lying sick of a fever in the wilds of Loch Ericht, seems, however, to show very clearly that Clough's *practice*, so far from being inferior to, was actually in advance of, his *teaching* :—that he not only was as strict with himself as he was with others, but that where his sense of right and justice pointed out that a certain act should be performed, he had the moral strength of character to at once go and do it. This is a great matter,—for the individual or nation that can not only see, but do, what is right and just, is gifted with both intelligence and virtue, those two qualities so closely allied that sometimes one can with difficulty distinguish between them.

It will, perhaps, be urged by some persons that although Clough's mind seems, indeed, to have been 'habitually swayed by large, slow, deep-sea currents,' yet that he had no special message of his own to deliver to mankind, no direct teaching to put forward, no assured gospel or tidings of any certainty, to proclaim to his hearers or readers. But those who might possibly be disposed to put aside or depreciate his poems in this manner, would plainly have mistaken for weakness what is the very soul, and strength, and essence, of Clough's poetry and power. The gospel which he proclaims, and which will be found either implied or directly stated in most of his compositions, is that

man cannot be saved by assertion, or by affirmation
of stereotyped beliefs,—but by growth, by progress,
by receptive flexibility of intellect, by a readiness
of mind to accept or consider fresh ideas, new truths,
increasing knowledge. This it is that constitutes
the positive element in Clough's teaching :—

> 'To gather facts from far and near,
> Upon the mind to hold them clear,
> And, knowing more may yet appear,
> Unto one's latest breath to fear
> The premature result to draw.'

Nor does, indeed, the positive element of his
poetry end here. It is carried on, and completed,
in several different directions, and of these one not
to be overlooked is that indicated by the words of
the German sage, *'Wen Gott betrügt, ist wohl
betrogen—whom God deludes is well deluded,'*—a
truth which in Clough's teaching is apparent in his
unceasing reverence, no less than in the absence of
the harsher forms of iconoclasm.

The first impression produced by the sight of
great mountains is said to be often one of disappointment in that their 'summits never seem so
near the sky as we had hoped to see them.' But as
soon as the eye and mind gradually compass and

comprehend the height and majesty of the object before them,—the topmost peaks of which, we perceive, do in truth mingle with the heavens and are hidden away in clouds of encircling mystery,— we discover that our disappointment in the first instance arose not from the insignificance of the object, but from our own incapacity, our own want of perception and comprehensiveness. It is to some extent also true that our impression on reading a poet's works for the first time is often one verging on disappointment. We cast a cursory glance over the pages, we read a verse or two here, and a line or two there, and thinking that we have compassed and fathomed the poet's work, and that we know his height and depth, his mass and substance, we lay down the book, we are disappointed. It is to be hoped that no readers will allow themselves to be thus disappointed with Clough until they have become thoroughly conversant with all his compositions, not only in verse but also in prose. In that case one can promise them with much confidence that in the end they will not be disappointed at all.

In conclusion it should be observed that in studying Clough's poems we should always remember what manner of man he was, we should call to mind those words of one of his dearest friends, Mr. C. E. Norton, who writes :—

' To win such love as Arthur Hugh Clough won in life, to leave so dear a memory as he has left, is a happiness that falls to few men. * * * * Liberal in sentiment, absolutely free from dogmatism and pride of intellect, of a questioning temper, but of reverent spirit, faithful to the performance not only of the larger duties, but also of the lesser charities and the familiar courtesies of life, he has left a memory of singular consistency, purity, and dignity.   He lived to conscience, not for show, and few men carry through life so white a soul.'

CHISWICK PRESS :—C. WHITTINGHAM AND CO. TOOKS COURT, CHANCERY LANE.